PSYCHOSOCIAL ASPECTS OF NUCLEAR DEVELOPMENTS

Report of the Task Force on Psychosocial Aspects of
Nuclear Developments of the
American Psychiatric Association

Rita R. Rogers, M.D., Chairperson
William Beardslee, M.D.
Doyle I. Carson, M.D.
Jerome Frank, M.D.
John Mack, M.D.
Michael Mufson, M.D.

Approved for publication by the Council on
International Affairs

Jack Weinberg, M.D., Chairperson
Charles A. Pinderhughes, M.D.
Alfred M. Freedman, M.D.
John Carleton, M.D.
Jules Masserman, M.D.
Lindbergh Sata, M.D.
John Buckman, M.D.
Rita R. Rogers, M.D.
Rodney C. Johnson, M.D.
Ellen Mercer, Staff Liaison

Publication authorized by the Board of Trustees,
December, 1981

AMERICAN PSYCHIATRIC ASSOCIATION
1700 18th Street, N.W.
Washington, D.C. 20009

Jack Weinberg, M.D., a past President of APA and Chairperson of the Council on International Affairs, died on March 1, 1982. He was an active and thoughtful participant in many of APA's international projects. His guidance and wise counsel on this report are appreciated.

CONTENTS

INTRODUCTION

Since problems created by the splitting of the atom impinge on all structures and functions of society, ranging from legal systems to weapons technology, their solutions require contributions from all scientific disciplines, among them psychiatry and psychology. In the last analysis, all political decisions are made by individuals or small groups. The initiatory act to use a weapon— whether it be to give the command, press the button, or pull the trigger—is the performance of an individual. To this extent, analysis of human motives and of group dynamics must have some relevance, and on this basis the Task Force on Psychosocial Aspects of Nuclear Developments offers its report. We have attempted here to speculate on the psychosocial context, not only of the arms race but of nuclear technology in general.

Nuclear weapons have called into serious question the continued viability of war as an instrument of national policy. Their unlimited destructive power and the radioactivity of the products of their explosions have created certain new threats, without any precedents in human history.

Psychiatrists struggle to resolve conflicts between their personal opinions, their professional scholarly identities, and their dedication to understanding human experience in all its dimensions. Indeed the task of psychiatry is to bridge the emotional and the cognitive, a task equally constant and arduous for the layperson struggling to understand the implications of nuclear developments in this extraordinary and trying age.

Also, the nuclear arms race aggravates some ominous features of human behavior: the inability to adjust perceived reality to actual reality rapidly enough when the latter abruptly changes; the propensity to resort to violence when frustrated or frightened; blind obedience; and the primitivizing effect of emotions on thought and on images of the enemy, with special reference to deterrence. All of this takes place in the context of a common realization that adequate defense against nuclear weapons is

v

neither practically nor theoretically possible. Thus, it is psychologically safest to distance the prospect of and fear of nuclear war.

Problems of this type have always existed, though never on so widespread a scale; but today they are aggravated by unprecedented circumstances. First is the mounting interdependence of nations so that unrest in any one threatens the stability of many. Second, which aggravates the first, is instantaneous, worldwide, electronic dissemination of information. But it is the advent of nuclear weapons that forces leaders of the nuclear powers to play a new game for enormous stakes, while at the same time having to create the rules—surely one of the most difficult problems national decision-makers have ever faced.

People of all nations today must cope with urgent and complex dilemmas, some old and some unprecedented. Under the stresses of overpopulation, energy shortages, crushing arms budgets, and other strains, the globe seems to be careening out of control. Unrest is mounting everywhere—in industrialized as well as non-industrialized areas, in communist and capitalist nations, on all continents. Increased repression, secrecy, torture, rebellion, and terrorism result from this unrest.

Nuclear technology, too, confronts people with profound psychological dilemmas, as we have learned from our review of the international literature and from our studies of the aftermath of the Three Mile Island accident. People are faced with a technology which can affect them profoundly but which they cannot fully understand. This creates emotional dissonance and uncertainty, anxieties and stress, and perhaps explains the interchangeable use of and reaction to the concepts of nuclear weapons and nuclear power. In some cases, these reactions lead to nearly total denial, what Robert Lifton termed "psychic shutdown" or "numbing", the phenomenon that leads the individual to refuse to consider the realities of the nuclear age, even though they affect his life intensely in immediate and long term ways.

As our colleagues in the Group for the Advancement of Psychiatry (GAP) observed in 1964, when they released their report on Psychiatric Aspects of the Prevention of Nuclear War, "We have not assumed that we could supply

any definitive answers. We can but make available whatever increments of understanding we achieve to those
who bear the awesome responsibility of decision." Since
1964 we hope we have gained more understanding in the
light of increased experience.

In the intervening years, many more nations have
developed nuclear destructive capability and those with
nuclear weapons, especially the United States and the
Soviet Union, have vastly increased the size and sophistication of their nuclear arsenals. Nuclear plant technology
is now purchasable by almost every nation on earth. In
the United States, as a result of the accident at Three
Mile Island, nuclear energy became gravely suspect in the
public mind.

The possibility of a nuclear accident, or indeed, of a
nuclear war, no longer seems remote. As a result of these
developments, we believe there now exists heightened
apprehension about the threat of nuclear attack and power
plant disaster. The charge to the Task Force, established
under the auspices of the A.P.A. Council on Emerging
Issues in 1977 at the urging of Perry Ottenberg, M.D. was
to bring psychological understanding to bear on various
aspects of the development of nuclear arms and nuclear
energy and the threat that they pose to human physical,
mental, and emotional life.

The Task Force included psychiatrists Rita R. Rogers,
M.D., Chairperson; William Beardslee, M.D., Doyle I.
Carson, M.D., Jerome Frank, M.D., John Mack, M.D., and
Michael Mufson, M.D. Dr. Ottenberg provided seminal
contributions and participated in the initial meetings.
Several consultants, expert in one aspect or another of the
problem, met with the Task Force, and special acknowl-
edgment of the valuable contribution of Jack Ruina,
Ph.D. of Massachusetts Institute of Technology is appropriate. The Task Force would also like to acknowledge
James Henning, Ph.D., a psychologist consultant who designed the questionnaire administered by Task Force
members, and credit in particular Michael Mufson, M.D.
who was assigned to the Task Force as a Falk Fellow and
who eventually assumed full membership as a result of his
diligent and valuable contributions.

In the chapters of its report, the Task Force has addressed the psychosocial aspects of the arms race, United

States-Soviet relations in the nuclear context, the emotional responses to nuclear issues and terrorism, the impact of nuclear developments on children and adolescents, the relationship of secrecy to nuclear developments, and the psychological aspects of the accident of Three Mile Island. Finally there is a review of the relevant literature.

We have tried to reflect on past work, our own and our colleagues, as well as to push ourselves forward into a world that might perhaps someday evolve a way for living without war, but with a truer understanding of the technology that has made a mammoth of the atom we cannot see.

As Lawrence Langer most eloquently stated in *The Age of Atrocity*, "To be in touch with the intolerable and to remain psychologically whole is the vexing challenge that confronts us. To ignore the intolerable, as if death by atrocity were an aberration and not a crucial fact of our mental life, is to pretend an innocence that history discredits and statistics defame. But it is easier to formulate this challenge than to face it."

Mindful that this report formulates as many challenges as it faces, we offer our work in the hope that it can contribute to the braver better world that is within the power of all humanity to fashion.

SOCIOPSYCHOLOGICAL ASPECTS OF THE NUCLEAR ARMS RACE

Jerome Frank, M.D.

Nuclear weapons demand more drastic and abrupt changes in national behavior as the price of survival than ever before in history. Because of their unprecedented destructive power, they are making obsolete the reliance on force or the threat of it as the ultimate source of security in international relations. The survival of Western civilization—perhaps the survival of humanity itself—now demands a fundamental revision in patterns of behavior that humans have relied on since men first banded together in hunting groups.

Humans respond to events as they perceive them, not necessarily as events occur in reality. Fortunately, perceived reality usually coincides closely enough with objective reality so that behavior does not become seriously maladaptive. Furthermore, thanks to humans' extraordinary powers of symbolization, when objective reality changes, they are usually able to adjust their perceptions and behavior sufficiently promptly to avoid disaster. When objective reality changes drastically and abruptly enough, however, especially when the changes create new and unprecedentedly severe threats that can be mastered only by radical changes in individual patterns of behavior and thinking, then a dangerous gap between perceived and objective reality may ensue.

In the days of spears and clubs and ordinary guns, there was no gap between the objective and perceived realities of weaponry. Weapons conferred strength upon their possessors, both in appearance and in fact. The image of strength projected by a large stockpile of non-nuclear weapons was based on real strength; therefore it was realistic for individuals or national leaders to rely on weapons to reassure themselves, intimidate their actual or potential enemies, and hold the loyalty of their allies.

Nuclear weapons have abruptly and permanently broken the connection between weaponry and strength in

1

one respect but not in another. Perceived and actual reality still coincide insofar as strategic nuclear weapons in the hands of one adversary gravely menace the other. They differ sharply beyond a certain point, however, in that the more a nation possesses, the stronger and more secure it and other nations perceive it to be, whereas in actuality the reverse is true.

Beyond a level long since passed by the U.S. and the U.S.S.R., accumulating more powerful and sophisticated strategic nuclear weapons increases the danger to all nations, including the possessor. It stimulates the spread of these weapons to nations that do not now possess them. It also assures that they will eventually fall into the hands of terrorists thereby increasing the probability of their being launched by accident or malice.

Nevertheless, since the nation that possesses fewer nuclear weapons appears weaker to itself and its allies, it will feel and act as if it actually were weaker; it will be more readily intimidated and be less assertive in pursuing its goals. This condition is a powerful and understandable impetus to the nuclear arms competition. It is also an important psychological source in the endless scenarios produced by all national leaders showing how their home country could prevail after a nuclear exchange. In this sense, building nuclear arsenals is an especially costly and dangerous form of psychological warfare.

The hope for achieving weapons superiority rests on the unwarranted extrapolation of conclusions from the realm of technology to that of human behavior. To be sure, science and technology have solved innumerable problems, including many long considered to be insoluble, such as splitting the atom and breaking the genetic code. But all such problems have been posed by nature, not by fellow humans, and therein lies their crucial difference from arms races. That is, although problems of military attack and defense present themselves as technological, their ultimate source lies in the minds of the adversary; each technological innovation by one side is sooner or later counteracted by the other.

With non-nuclear weapons, technological superiority has been occasionally achieved, but because of the rapidity of technological advance these periods of superiority have become ever briefer. The relative duration of the supremacy of cavalry, tanks, and the Stuka dive bomber come to mind. Today there is practically no lag because technological knowledge is so rapidly diffused.

Nevertheless, leaders of technologically advanced nations continue to pursue the will-o'-the-wisp of technological superiority, motivated in part by a belief in the power of deterrence, to be discussed later, and in part by the fear that a rival might just possibly achieve a breakthrough which would tempt it to attack by enabling it, even for a very brief period, to do so with relative impunity. The more feverish the pace of research and development, the greater the mutual fear of attack.

Leaders of all nuclear nations stress the immeasurable catastrophe that a strategic nuclear exchange would cause. Yet they continue to prepare for such an exchange. The understanding of this paradox requires broadening the focus to include three biologically and phylogenetically rooted aspects of human nature: the propensity to resort to violence when frightened or frustrated, submission to authority, and the priority of group needs over those of the individual.

It must be emphasized at this point that there is no direct link between biological properties of humans and their social behavior. The expression of biological needs in every society is channeled and shaped by cultural values and institutions. Because of the unique human capacity to symbolize, humans can satisfy biological urges in a huge variety of ways. Hence, although biological needs cannot be ignored, biology is not destiny.

A good example relevant to understanding the paradox of preparing for nuclear exchange is the stimulation of the impulse to violence by threat or frustration—a reaction common to all vertebrates and necessary for biological survival. In humans, the subjective response to such a challenge is anger or fear; the objective response is an effort to destroy the threatener or at least to render it harmless. This restores the sense of safety and enhances the victor's own sense of power.

Since humans are self-aggrandizing, they will always push against their environment until they come up against frustrating or frightening obstacles, human or otherwise; so instigators to violence are omnipresent. Although it is undeniable that programs of violence are im-

3

bedded in the human central nervous system, there is no direct link between them and complex social behaviors such as waging war. Innate patterns of scratching, biting, and kicking have nothing to do with launching a nuclear missile. Waging war must be learned afresh by every generation. In this sense war is only thirty years old. To claim that because man is innately violent, war is inevitable is like concluding that because he is violent, human sacrifice in religious rites is inevitable, or that because man is innately carnivorous, cannibalism is inevitable. Human survival, to be sure, now demands the creation of less lethal psychological equivalents for war, but in principle this is not beyond the bounds of possibility.

Two other deeply ingrained patterns which humans share with all social creatures are obedience and readiness to sacrifice the individual to preserve the group.

The stability of all organized societies, animal and human, rests on a hierarchy of power. Members of even the most democratic human societies unhesitatingly obey legitimate authority. This was elegantly, if somewhat horrifyingly, demonstrated by a well-known experiment in which the experimenter told normal American male adults that the experiment for which they had volunteered required them to deliver painful, possibly lethal shocks to an inoffensive stranger. About two-thirds of the subjects carried out these orders. (The victim, of course, was an accomplice; he received no shocks.) The most disquieting findings were that the more remote the victim, and the more the responsibility for delivering the shock was shared, the greater the obedience. When the subject had only to throw a master switch that permitted someone else to give the shock, more than 90 percent complied.[1] This is uncomfortably analogous to the circumstances under which a nuclear missile would be launched. The enemy is physically and psychologically remote, and one person cannot launch it alone. So it should not be surprising that when the commander of a Polaris submarine was asked how it felt to be the man whose act could unleash the submarine's destructive power, he replied: "I've never given it any thought, but if we ever have to hit, we'll hit and there won't be a second's hesitation."[2]

Obedience may be a much more dangerous threat to survival than the propensity to violence. The predominant emotion of soldiers in a missile bunker or a nuclear submarine is boredom. As the above quotation implies, they would fire the weapon simply because they were ordered to do so.

As already suggested, obedience is rooted in the fact that humans can survive only as members of organized groups; hence survival of the group takes precedence over survival of the individual. Ants, baboons, and humans are all prepared to sacrifice their individual lives to save their groups.

Groups provide protection against hostile environments and outside enemies. They also engender a sense of psychological security in that, since all members share the same customs and norms, they can predict each other's behavior, and the group carries the values that give meaning and significance to their lives. Groups are psychologically extensions of their members so a threat to the group's integrity strikes at the very basis of both their biological and their psychological existence.

This may in part explain the paradoxical behavior of leaders of nuclear powers. Their justification for preparing for a catastrophe they know should be avoided at all costs is that the best protection against a nuclear holocaust is to be able to inflict it on the enemy if necessary—an extension of the policy of deterrence, refuted by all the lessons of pre-nuclear history, as will be discussed below. A more plausible although unstated reason is that, although everyone dreads death in nuclear war, they dread even more the threat to the nation's physical and psychological survival posed by an enemy victory—summed up in the slogan, "Better dead than Red."

Humans share with all social animals the predisposition to fear and distrust members of groups other than their own. When two groups compete for the same goal, this distrust rapidly escalates into what has been called the image of the enemy. It is remarkable how similar this image is no matter who the conflicting parties are. Enemy images mirror each other—that is, each side attributes the same virtues to itself and the same vices to the enemy. "We" are trustworthy, peace-loving, honorable, and humanitarian; "they" are treacherous and warlike. As successive Gallup polls have shown, Americans used the last two adjectives to characterize Germans, Russians,

Japanese, and Chinese only when they were enemies. The words promptly disappeared when these nations became friends.[3]

The image of the enemy impedes resolution of conflict in several ways. It creates a self-fulfilling prophecy by causing enemies to acquire the evil characteristics they attribute to each other. In combatting what they perceive to be the other's warlikeness and treachery, each side becomes more warlike and treacherous itself. As a result, the enemy image nations form of each other more or less corresponds to reality. Although the behavior of an enemy may be motivated by fear more than by aggressiveness, the nation that fails to recognize an enemy as treacherous and warlike would not long survive.

The image of the enemy as malevolent and untrustworthy leads to progressive restriction of communication until virtually the only messages that get through are those that reinforce the image, resulting in further restrictions— an ominous, vicious circle. The accompanying fear and hate create emotional tension. This facilitates oversimplification of thought, one feature of which is the *strain to consistency*. Since the enemy by definition is bad, *all* its actions are interpreted as motivated by malevolence. For example, United States officials perceived Soviet withdrawal of some troops from East Germany as a ruse to persuade the United States not to supply NATO with tactical weapons. The possibility that it might have been a genuine effort to reduce tension seems not even to have been entertained, because this would require a more differentiated view of Soviet motives.

The image of the enemy, moreover, results in a failure of empathy, manifested by an attacker's underestimation of the target's determination to resist. This may be a major psychological source of war.[4]

Faced with an adversary preceived as treacherous and implacably malevolent in a world without effective international peace-keeping institutions, a nation's only recourse is to confront the enemy with superior force in the hope that this will *deter* hostile acts through the threat of retaliation or defeat should deterrence fail.

Since resorting to nuclear weapons would be suicidal, nuclear powers are forced to rely on the hope of maintaining deterrence indefinitely. There are strong psychological grounds for believing that such a hope will continue to be vain in the future, as it always has been in the past.

Mutual deterrence between powers roughly equal in strength has always culminated in war. Deterrence breaks down when one of the parties calculates, correctly or incorrectly, that the potential benefits of the forbidden action outweigh the probable costs, as seen in Hitler's invasion of Poland; or when the emotional tensions that mutual deterrence always generates reach such a pitch that leaders stop calculating and throw caution to the winds. Thus, at the onset of World War I the Kaiser said, "Even if we are bled to death, England will at least lose India," and in ordering the attack on Pearl Harbor, the Japanese war minister said, "Once in a while it is necessary to close one's eyes and jump from the stage of the Kiyomizo Temple" (a favorite Japanese form of suicide).[5] This is the point when, as Bertrand Russell put it, the desire to destroy the enemy becomes greater than the desire to stay alive oneself.

Since meaningful superiority in nuclear weapons is objectively unattainable, deterrence has come to rely primarily on projecting an image of strength and resolution to the deterring nation itself, its allies, and its enemies. This includes proclaiming determination to launch a nuclear war if necessary. As Walt Rostow wrote: "Credible deterrence in the nuclear age lies in being prepared to face the consequences if deterrence fails—up to and including all-out nuclear war."[6] Since all-out nuclear war would be an immeasurable disaster, nuclear deterrence puts a premium on bluffing. Former Secretary of State Henry Kissinger wrote (before he entered politics, to be sure): "Deterrence depends above all on psychological criteria. . . . For purposes of deterrence a bluff taken seriously is more useful than a serious threat interpreted as a bluff."[7] Thus, each nuclear power is faced with the virtually impossible task of trying to make credible an essentially incredible threat.

Recently technological advances in the power and accuracy of intercontinental ballistic missiles have caused a shift from deterring an adversary by threatening to destroy his cities to threatening to destroy military targets. By putting a premium on striking first, thereby shortening decision time, nations intensify mutual fears and the danger of triggering a nuclear holocaust through accident or misjudgment.

In the grip of strong emotions, a person's thinking becomes more primitive—that is, he perceives fewer alternatives, simplifies issues, and focuses exclusively on combatting the immediate threat without considering remote or long-term consequences. Strong emotion also impels to impulsive action. There is nothing harder when under emotional stress than to do nothing.[8]

History is littered with the remains of societies whose leaders' judgment failed under emotional pressure. As Robert Kennedy indicated in his book on the Cuban missile crisis, even some of the "best and brightest" can reach a breaking point: ". . .some [of the decision-makers] because of the pressure of events, even appeared to lose their judgment and stability."[9]

The fact that major decisions concerning national policy are made by small groups rather than individuals does not protect these decisions from irrationality. On the contrary, groups may be more prone to rash actions under some circumstances than individuals. To be sure, a group has access to information from more sources and affords opportunities to express more viewpoints, which should help steady its judgments, and a group member may be restrained by others who do not share his perspective; but group members may also reinforce each other, or even egg each other on, especially if emotion runs high. This mutual reinforcement is strengthened by what Janis has termed "group-think."[10] The more a group feels threatened, the more its members are impelled to maintain group solidarity by agreeing with each other and the leader, even at the expense of their objective judgments. The Bay of Pigs invasion is an instructive example.

So much for some of the psychological aspects of the threats to survival created by nuclear weapons. Since from now on any war can escalate into a nuclear one, the only *ultimate* resolution of these threats requires the eventual creation of a world system without war. And there are a few slim grounds for hope.

Nuclear weapons themselves create intense pressures to continue negotiations in the midst of confrontation. While deterrence between equal powers has always failed, a stronger nation can usually deter a weaker one. Nuclear weapons have placed both adversaries in the position of the weaker one—that is, like the weaker adversary in pre-nuclear days, they run the grave risk of being destroyed as organized societies in a nuclear exchange, so they have no choice but to continue to negotiate.

Even if unsuccessful, the mere process of negotiation forces the parties to search for areas of agreement or compromise, as a result of which they form more differentiated perceptions of each other. Moreover, the longer negotiations continue, the more the parties form habits of behavior that counteract those of violence. Thus negotiations tend to weaken the mutual image of a monolithic enemy.

Treaties produced by negotiations, while they have not slowed the nuclear arms race, have regularized some of its aspects. To the extent that they eliminate some options, safeguard verification procedures, and set the form of the arms race, they reduce uncertainty as to the adversary's intentions and acts, a major source of mutual fear. Furthermore, the achievement of any treaty facilitates the next one and fans what few embers of trust there may be. Negotiations could in time reduce the emotional tension of national leaders to a level that would stimulate, rather than inhibit, the creation of the new solutions required to assure survival.

Given the depth and power of the psychosocial forces pushing national leaders to war, however, successful adjustment to a world in which war has ceased to be a viable arbiter of international conflict must be very slow at best. In the meanwhile, the discharge of at least one major nuclear weapon by accident or design seems virtually inevitable. Perhaps the resulting shock will accelerate the process of adaptation.

In the long term, strengthened international agencies might foster a heightened worldwide consciousness of the dangers of nuclear weapons. Nations need to be freed of the fear of one another, and recognition must be promoted that all peoples inhabit the same fragile spaceship.

References

1. Milgram S: Obedience to Authority. New York, Harper and Row, 1974

2. Cary WH Jr: Madmen at Work: The Polaris Story. Philadelphia, PA, American Friends Service Committee, undated
3. The Gallup Poll: Image of red powers. The Santa Barbara News Press, June 26, 1966
4. White RK: Absence of empathy—a major cause of war? Political Psychology 3, 1981 (in press)
5. Holsti OR: The value of international tension measurements. Journal of Conflict Resolution 7:611, 1963
6. Rostow WW: The test: are we the tougher? New York Times Magazine, June 7, 1964, pp 112-3
7. Kissinger HA: Central issues in American foreign policy in Agenda for the Nation. Edited by Gordon K. Garden City, NY, Doubleday and Co, 1968
8. Group for the Advancement of Psychiatry: Psychiatric Aspects of Nuclear War, Report 57. New York, 1964, pp 237-240
9. Kennedy RF: Thirteen Days. New York, WW Norton, 1969, p 31
10. Janis IL, Mann L: Decision Making: A Psychological Analysis of Conflict, Choice & Commitment. New York, Free Press, 1977

ON EMOTIONAL RESPONSES TO NUCLEAR ISSUES AND TERRORISM*

Rita R. Rogers, M.D.

As Chairperson of the Task Force on the Psychosocial Aspects of Nuclear Developments of the American Psychiatric Association, I became involved in a series of investigations concerning the human dimensions in nuclear issues. As I conducted interviews and examined the subjects' perceptions of nuclear issues and compared them with my own, I was struck not only by the difficulty of obtaining data concerning responses, but more so by the reluctance and indeed inability of interviewees and interviewers to get involved in the questions of nuclear issues. It was almost as if human contact became diminished or even nonexistent when one addressed the subject of nuclear danger. Interviewers and interviewees seemed constrained from becoming involved with the subject and with each other. The people interviewed shrugged their shoulders, continued their activities, remained uninvolved, and the dialogue ceased. There was no anger, displacement, or resentment about being asked; there was only nothingness and uninvolvement. Comparing this seeming "nebulousness" with interviews I had conducted concerning emotional climates in various nationalistic and conflicted relationships—Arab-Israeli[1] Pakistani-Bangladesh, and Turkish-Greek in Cyprus—I was struck by *how* participatory, emotionally involved, interested, agitated, and fierce people of the respective groups had been when they talked about their sides and their realities, and the manner in which they had presented their justifications, rationalizations, projections, distortions, displacements, and, in some cases, their vulnerabilities. In discussions of terrorism I found, in myself and my

*This article appeared in The Psychiatric Journal of the University of Ottawa, 5, no 3:147-152, September 1980.

subjects, fierce participation, involvement, preoccupa- tion, attention; projection into the event of one's own intentions, motives, outcomes; and displacement of anger, regardless of how informed or uninformed the par- ticipants were.

Both terrorism and nuclear issues are psychosocial emerging issues of our times. Why did I perceive in my- self and encounter in my subjects such an overwhelming difference in response to these topics? Why were we com- pelled to devour every article and report about highjack- ing and terrorism no matter how far away they had oc- curred and who had been involved? We seemed to have an inordinate involvement, hunger, preoccupation, and emotional readiness to respond to the sensationalism of terrorism. Why? And why, seemingly, did I and my sub- jects "turn-off" from nuclear issues? In fact, neither the term "turn-off" nor "turn-away" seemed to fit. There seemed to exist no adequate term. The response to the impact of nuclear issues on our psychosocial perceptions apparently does not fit into our psychosocial framework. The responses were not ones of denial, projection, ration- alization, reaction formation, intellectualization, or dis- placement. Rather, the response was "nothing." It was almost as though we humans had no emotional platform within ourselves on which to place these issues. Was there a connection between the "nothing" response to nuclear issues and the exaggerated response to terrorism?

In an attempt to find some understanding of the re- lationship between the self and collective self, and the relationship to one's *Menschlichkeit*, the following ques- tions were asked of a random sample of fifty people:

Do you ever think of nuclear issues?
What do you think about them?
Do you think there might be a nuclear war?
If the answer was "no," why not?
What would you do if there were one?
What do you think about terrorists getting hold of a
    nuclear bomb?
Is it likely? How come? What should one do about it?
If the answer was "no," why not?
What about the future?
Can you imagine any of it?

Do you dream about it?
Do your children ask about nuclear issues? What do
you tell them?
What should one tell them?
What should one do about it?
Do your children talk about it? With each other? With
you?
Do your children talk about terrorism? What do you
tell them?

Impressions

These questions were asked of a random population
sample which lacked controls. The informality in questioning and, most of all, the quality of the responses,
especially the unease that developed in interviewer and
interviewees, made tabulation of the questions and responses appear worthless but the lack of responses elicited some soul-searching questions.

The people interrogated were of different ages and
came from different walks of life: a seamstress, a psychia-
trist, a hairdresser, a librarian, a carpenter, etc. There
were more women than men, a number were psychiatric
outpatients, and some, but not all, had something in common with one another. They did not resent the questions,
they were not startled by them, but they considered them
bizarre. The patients whom I interviewed were less reluc-
tant to get involved with the questions than were the
non-patients. Obviously, they felt that their therapist
could ask them anything. Their willingness to become
engaged with the questions had to do with their willingness to be involved with the questioner (the therapist),
rather than any quality of the questions themselves. In the
psychiatric outpatients, however, the blandness of their
responses to these questions was noteworthy in comparison to their responses to the movies *Roots* and *Sybil*,[2]
which involved strong personal projections and inter-
weaving the themes of the movies with their personal
priorities and experiences. Indeed, these movies had been
viewed almost exclusively through the prism of their personal experiences. Not so in the case of nuclear issues! The
comparison, of course, is somewhat unfair because the

13

movies had had a visual impact which catapulted personal images into the forefront. Nuclear issues, however, could not be viewed, touched, smelled, heard, sensed, or imagined.

The non-patient subjects responded in a more baffled, nonresponsive way. They were less trusting than the patients. The seamstress stopped for a moment and with a needle between her teeth said, "Do you think about such things?" Her tone of voice expressed doubt about the person asking the question. The cosmetologist replied, "These are not issues we think about. Do you? How come?" The wife of a physician said, "I used to worry about it in the '50s when there was all that talk about bomb shelters, but now I don't." The social worker replied, "There is no economic profit in nuclear warfare, therefore there won't be any." The high school student said, "Since nobody can win, nobody will do anything about it." The hairdresser replied, "These are not things for our concern, let the politicians worry about it." The same hairdresser, however, reported that the most thrilling experience during his four-week trip to Europe in the spring was the moment he heard in Milan, Italy, that they had found Aldo Moro's body. This hairdresser knew nothing about politics, Italy, Europe, or terrorists, but he could feel the electrical excitement of the Italian people and their participation in the victimization of Aldo Moro. Why could the fate of one man at the hands of terrorists incite such a deep sense of involvement in a bystander from another country, while the possibility of the destruction of the world seemingly cannot elicit either interest or concern, or, most of all, involvement?

Nuclear Issues and Limits of Human Fantasy

It is difficult to find answers. Gunter Anders, in his paper "Reflections on the H-Bomb,"[3] asked in-depth questions about the meaning of the hydrogen bomb. He argued that nuclear issues have profoundly altered the reservoir of human fantasies. In his words, "Man's capacity for action has outgrown his emotional, imaginative, and moral capacities." Anders poignantly argued that we are incapable of producing a fear commensurate with the

H-bomb threat, let alone of constantly maintaining it in the midst of our still seemingly normal everyday life. He ascribed this to the limitations of our psyche, and said, "We have scruples about murdering one man; we have less scruples about shooting a hundred men; and no scruples at all about bombing a city out of existence. A city full of dead people remains a mere word for us." The infinite power man has acquired in the nuclear age has, according to Anders, reversed all history to prehistory and has changed the same anatomical creature into a new species. By altering history and the future, the present possibly gains a different meaning, or becomes meaningless.

We have to ask ourselves how this influences intergenerational relationships and through them our dependence and independence. This infinite power, the power to destroy the world, might be so intoxicating that one can no longer face or conceive of one's boundaries and limits. It possibly blurs the concepts of the self and the interaction of the self with other groups and with the world. By implication, the concept of *we* denotes mankind. What has this infinite power done to our *we* concept? Does a *we* include a world we can destroy? The word "compassion" demands a different *we* concept. Our feelings of dependence and independence are intimately interwoven with the symbolic meanings of child, parent, and relatives, namely the intertwining of past and future with the present functioning as moderator between these two. Prelife, life, death, and postdeath have always been interwoven. Now the *present* glares out, uncushioned by the memories of the past and devoid of the future.

Anders stated that the extermination camps, founded on the idea that all men are exterminable, were the precursors of the nuclear age. The idea of the nuclear age, according to Anders, is that all *mankind* is exterminable, the culmination of historical development as follows:

1. All men are mortal.
2. All men are exterminable.
3. All mankind is exterminable.

The traditional mortality-immortality stance has been profoundly altered. Our style of dealing with the issue of mortality and our fantasy of immortality used to be dealt with through such defenses as creativity, fame, fear (especially fear of death), memories, daydreams, fantasies, and most importantly, having children. We frequently skew the past to fit our future aspirations. We use action and inaction to soothe our anxieties and to help us deal with not wanting to face our own mortality. It is possible that we find ourselves incapable of thinking, feeling, or contemplating nuclear issues because the detonation of the nuclear bomb may be considered not an *action,* but an *inaction,* at least something which does not elicit our participation or involvement.

Action and Counteraction

Our hyperinvolvement with terrorism, that is, our willingness to be the participatory audience for terrorism (and terrorism depends on having an audience), is related to its offering us an opportunity to be shocked and outraged and to see and imagine action and counteraction. It gives us an opportunity for intense moral reactions of *ought* and *ought not.*

While the nuclear threat seems to derive from machines—at least that is how we perceive it—terrorism comes brutally from humans. We seem to read with hunger all the details about the backgrounds of the terrorists and their values. We look at photographs of terrorists and their victims, and news reports responsive to the cravings of the readers publish pictures of the terrorists before and after they become terrorists.[4] The terrorists, responsive to the cravings of the audience and attuned to their needs, send out pictures, tapes, and messages from the victims. Terrorists and victims reach us directly through our antennae, through our senses. We hear the messages, we see the drama, we fantasize the event and project into it our most sadistic and destructive cravings. We reach above it with our most exalted countermeasures; we imagine ourselves rescuing the victims. Acts of terrorism also offer us an unusual flexibility for our *we* feelings. Terrorists can be patriots or murderers depending on what our *we* feeling needs are. For example, a young Russian immigrant engineer, talking accusingly about Palestinian hijackers as murderers, on the same day referred to some Russians who attempted to hijack a plane, as supermen-patriots who risked their lives for mankind!

Terrorism Is Theater

Terrorism is directly perceived. It offers an exercise in elasticity to our moral and social fiber. Nuclear threats cannot be grasped; terrorism can. Nuclear issues do not rouse a sense of accountability, while terrorism offers an outlet for magnificent and accumulated outrage. We feel that we could never shake hands with a terrorist or put flowers in his path if our collective selves were to demand of us to call him a hero. But we could shake hands with the perpetrator of a nuclear act. In Anders' words, "Such a man suffers from an internal innocence, after all there are only co-agents in the nuclear world." Nobody is completely active; everybody is half active and half passive. Their activities are outside the realm of moral indignation. But the actions of terrorist agents fall within the realm of familiar standards. We can imagine the victim in a closet or in the trunk of a car. The crude message from the victim raises gut reactions as does the voice on the tape. These messages penetrate our emotional arena; we are there.

Brian Michael Jenkins defined terrorism as violence "calculated to inspire fear, to create an atmosphere of alarm which in turn causes people to exaggerate the strength of the terrorists and the importance of their cause. Since most terrorist groups are small and have few resources, the violence they carry out must be deliberately shocking. Terrorism is violence choreographed for its effect on an audience. Terrorism is theatre."[5] The effect of this violence lies in our readiness, capacity, and hunger for catapulting our needs into this human interaction. The nuclear threat, however, in spite of its existence and our cognitive awareness of it, does not penetrate our human fantasy. It remains there and we here. We see it as in another realm.

Victims and Victimizers

In nuclear issues we cannot imagine ourselves as either the *victim* or the *victimizer*. A terrorist act offers us an opportunity to feel ourselves in either role (according to our official allegiances and buried needs). Nuclear threats cannot be classified into good or bad, while terrorism offers us an opportunity for stark splitting into good and

17

bad and the flexibility to convert some terrorists into heroes and some into gangsters. This, in turn, offers us an opportunity for linkages with our group feelings. We can extend our *we* feelings to our parents, ancestors, and children, and in this way gain increased feelings of security and certainty. Nuclear issues are nebulous and decrease our perceptions of life, the world, and our boundaries. Linkages to ancestors and progeny are nonexistent. Our lives possibly become more "now" oriented, more hedonistic, more frantic and also more diminished in feelings. While the brutality of a terrorist act stimulates primitive excitement, the nuclear threat creates only a feeling of bland, nonparticipatory aloofness. The threat exceeds the boundaries of our emotional capacities. The terrorist act fills us not only with excitement but also prompts a reversion to our primitive anxieties. We re-experience the whole scale of human emotion from dreadful fear to pity, projective identification, identification with the aggressor, anguish, and anger toward the aggressor. We embrace the feelings of the victim, and we experience the anguish of the victim's family. We can sense the sadism of the terrorists. In fact, we even have an opportunity for a boundless unleashing of antiterrorist measures.

Terrorism and Outrage

While nuclear issues evoke a freezing point of human dimensions, terrorism provokes intense human participation. We have no armament, linguistically, intellectually, or emotionally, for dealing with nuclear issues. But terrorism offers us catharsis for pent-up outrage and channels for camouflaging personal hurts behind group interest. While we have no moral imagination for nuclear issues, terrorism gives us an opportunity for moral indignation behind which we can hide from ourselves our most primitive needs for cruelty and destruction. Nuclear threats rob us of our human calendar; there is no yesterday, today, or tomorrow. The terrorist act simplifies time concepts for us; the terrorists set a deadline—till Sunday at 2:00 P.M. This time element is broadcast by radio and television. We feel united with the world, waiting for the message from the terrorists or from the victim. This sensational waiting for the deadline takes us away from our daily preoccupations. We become participants in something bigger than our daily lives.

But nuclear threats are too big for our participation. Perpetrators of nuclear acts could be law-abiding citizens, scholars, scientists, or technicians. We cannot imagine them as being brutal. They take us back to our childhood fears and eerie fairytales. The terrorists wear masks. Terrorists may be on the fringes of sanity. They are involved in a human-to-human brutality that makes them akin to us. We can judge them by our internal principles which we can turn off and on. But we have no internal principles for judging nuclear developments. Nuclear confrontations are reserved for the giant-to-giant interactions of the superpowers. These are unthinkable, unimaginable conflicts. Their rivalries are transposed and transferred into circumscribed areas: the Middle East, Africa, wherever. These local conflicts elicit new military technology, guerrilla warfare, and terrorist activity; and it is here that the dangerous, potential confluence between nuclear warfare and terrorist activity might occur—in the surrogate warfares of small groups which bear open, gaping wounds of emotional group vulnerabilities.

Nuclear Terrorism

Will terrorists go nuclear? In a publication of the same name, Brian Jenkins addressed himself to this question. He felt that "the rapid growth of a civilian nuclear industry and increasing traffic in plutonium, enriched uranium and radioactive waste material, the spread of nuclear technology both in the United States and abroad, all increase the opportunities for terrorists to engage in some type of 'nuclear action.' "[6]

In the same study Jenkins expressed the opinion that the virtual guarantee of widespread publicity may increase the possibilities that terrorists will go nuclear. "Going nuclear" would enhance the dramatic effect of terrorism and, in Jenkins' words, "the basic theory of terrorism—violence to gain attention, instill fear, and thereby gain political leverage—nuclear blackmail would seem to be, at least in theory, extremely attractive to terrorists."[7]

19

At this point, it is important to consider Frederick J. Hacker's differentiation of terrorists into "Crusaders, Criminals, and Crazies."[8] The criminals or mercenaries whose interest is in the ransom (no matter what means are used to get it), would be inclined to use nuclear threats (often hoaxes) to convince their audience to render what they want.

The crazies, in most likelihood, would welcome the aggrandizement the nuclear threat would give them in their own eyes and their audience's. The concept "nuclear" might mesh with their feelings of lack of boundaries, lack of bonds, and depersonalization. Because of the distance which psychotic patients experience between themselves and other people, nuclear bomb threats might be perceived as welcome distances from the rest of the people. The introduction of an unimaginable and intangible nuclear object "between themselves and these others" would be welcomed as a safeguard by paranoid patients who fear intrusion of others upon themselves.

The enigma, potency, sinister aspects, and lack of humaneness of nuclear devices could be dangerously appealing to psychotic patients. Also in terms of identification, it might be easier for a psychotic patient to identify with a nuclear bomb than with a father, teacher, or other powerful figure. Here one is reminded of the tragic way in which an autistic child (if he can talk) might reply that when he grows up he wants to be a windshield wiper—not a policeman, fireman, or pilot, as other children might choose, but rather an inanimate object engaged in a repetitive, stereotypic motion.

The chilled response elicited by the word "nuclear" might have special appeal to Hacker's crusaders.[8] The terrorists who want to draw attention to themselves and their causes by creating alarm, could be increasingly drawn to the nuclear "prop" which would gain for them worldwide attention.

Jenkins argued that the scenarios for the deliberate dispersal of toxic radioactive material, which would cause a number of immediate deaths, a greater number of serious and protracted illnesses, a statistical rise in the mortality rate, and ultimately an increase in the number of birth defects among the affected population, do not appear to fit the patterns of terrorist actions carried out thus far.[9]

Terrorism needs an arena and an audience, and the nuclear bomb might not appeal to the "crusader" terrorist because it would destroy the arena along with the audience. Nuclear rivalry could be considered an unimaginable competition of the superpowers, distant and inaccessible. Terrorists are usually involved in surrogate wars of the superpowers in local conflicts, the imaginable ones, the ones which touch our old-fashioned nationalist, ethnic, small-group feelings. We have no concept of time for the balance of terror. There is no sound, no framework for our "memories." The terrorists' call for execution of the victim at 2:00 P.M., with the victim's voice on tape and picture in the newspaper, invites our participation in the drama. Parents and children can be united in fear, outrage, allegiance, prejudice, group, nation, and peoplehood feelings. These feelings, precipitated by threats of terrorism, can increase feelings of selfhood. There are no innocent bystanders in terrorism.

Yet, despite Jenkins' argument that nuclear weapons are not appropriate to the style and aims of terrorists, we have to concern ourselves about their potential special emotional appeal for people of the underdeveloped world and dissident groups for strengthening their stance toward the superpowers. Because of desperate feelings of helplessness and dependence vis-a-vis the superpowers, lack of parity with them, and misrepresentations (voting and membership equality in the United Nations, for example) it might appeal to crusaders to acquire the superpowers' most exclusive supremacy symbol, nuclear weapons. Psychologically, the appeal might lie in the use of the weapons as symbols of defiance and/or pretensions of being as powerful as the superpowers.

When we contemplate the possibility of terrorists going nuclear, we must acknowledge the present-day political realities, which have produced an increase in local conflicts with imposed settlements (cease fires) rather than surrenders. Thus terrorism for political causes has increased because conflicted relationships have been kept simmering. These repetitive wars at relatively short intervals increase opportunities for simmering hurts and causes to be taken up by terrorists. The Arabs and Israelis who fought in 1948, 1956, 1967, and 1973; the Indians and Pakistanis who fought in 1947, 1965, and 1971; and the Cypriots, Turks, and Greeks who fought in 1963 and 1974 are all raising children and grandchildren who suffer from group hurts. Will the helplessness of their hurt prompt them to reach out toward that which makes us all feel equally helpless—the nuclear threat? We don't know.

One interesting phenomenon is that the children of hurt groups seem to feel an inordinate need to redress the perceived hurt of their parents. The Moluccan and Palestinian terrorists are youngsters who have never seen the homeland that they so fiercely and desperately claim. For example, oranges from Jaffa become bigger than life not for the refugee from Jaffa, Palestine, but for his son, and more so his grandson, who has never seen Jaffa. He seems to react to having to fight for a dream he has never been able to dream. His parents' hurt becomes interwoven with his basic anxieties of desertion, loss of love, and castration. Such youngsters seem to have more resentment for their parents' helplessness than for those whom the parents describe to them as aggressors. The virulence with which they fight for "their ancestors' causes" becomes fierce and brutal because of the lack of opportunity for reality testing.[10]

In the act of terrorism the audience participates in the threats to the victims' most basic anxieties. The contamination of fear is based on the ability of the audience (the world) to participate in regression with the victim and/or the victimizer. Terrorism uses the same appeal as fairy tales. There is danger that our increased adeptness at weaving nuclear realities into our fairy tales, movies, and other make believes, might bring them more into the realm of our emotional platform. Will this increase the appeal of nuclear threats for terrorists? Jenkins argued that the possible employers of terrorism are anti-nuclear extremists whose primary objective would be to halt all nuclear programs. He stated, "For example, a fanatical environmentalist might steal radioactive waste material and use it to secretly pollute a waterway, then blame the contamination on a nearby reactor. Several incidents have already occurred in which the perpetrators were known or suspected to be foes of nuclear power."[11] This statement corroborates the possibility that Hacker's crusaders could go nuclear. People with a fierce cause could find a special appeal in "going nuclear" to enhance their power.

Jenkins also stated that two-thirds of the present world population have never known a world which did not have poised nuclear missiles. Nuclear weapons have permeated our conceptual framework; they are part of us and not perceived as a foreign body. The new nuclear world is considered utopian.[12] Lewis Christian Bohn stressed that even SALT talks only about "stabilization" and "diminution."[13]

It seems that nuclear advances have penetrated all aspects of our lives without our being aware and without our building up defenses, rationalization, and denials. While terrorism as it is practiced today deals with ultimate repair, correction, and coercion, the consequences of nuclear wars are irreparable, and there is no need to think about afterwards.[14] Thus, we must ask ourselves: Is there a relationship between our present oriented society and the irreparability of nuclear war? Has man outgrown himself?

References

1. Rogers RR: The emotional climate in Israeli society. Am J Psychiatry 128:988-992, 1972
   Rogers RR: Self-involvement in the Middle East conflict. Committee on International Relations, Group for the Advancement of Psychiatry, New York, 1978
2. Rogers RR: Intergenerational exchange: transferences of attitudes down the generations, in Modern Perspectives in the Psychiatry of Infants. Edited by Howells J. New York, Brunner/Mazel, 1978
3. Anders G: Reflections on the H-bomb, in Moral Issues and Christian Response. Edited by Jersild PT, Johnson DA. New York, Holt, Rinehart and Winston, 1971, pp 334-342
4. Bradshaw J: The dream of terror. Esquire 90:25-50, 1978
5. Jenkins BM: High Technology Terrorism and Surrogate War: The Impact of New Technology on Low-level Violence. Santa Monica, CA, The Rand Corporation, 1975, p 338
6. Jenkins BM: Will Terrorists Go Nuclear? Santa Monica, CA, The Rand Corporation, 1975, p 6
7. *Ibid*, p 4
8. Hacker FJ: Crusaders, Criminals and Crazies. New York, WW Norton, 1976
9. Jenkins BM: Terrorism and the Nuclear Safeguards Issue. Santa Monica, CA, The Rand Corporation, 1975

10. Rogers RR: The emotional contamination between parent and children. Am J Psychiatry 36:267-271, 1976
11. Jenkins BM: Will Terrorists Go Nuclear? p 7
12. *Ibid*
13. Bohn LC: Nuclear deterrence: living by the bomb. New York Times, May 31, 1978
14. Weisskopf VF: A race to death. New York Times, May 14, 1978

SOVIET-AMERICAN RELATIONSHIPS UNDER THE NUCLEAR UMBRELLA

Rita R. Rogers, M.D.

Nuclear weapons involve the United States and the Soviet Union in a unique relationship which beckons psychiatric inquiry. Both possess weapons that they cannot use, but both consider the need for such weapons unavoidable. They perceive and measure each other's power in terms of nuclear weapons, but these weapons also remind them of their basic powerlessness and that their future is doomed through these weapons. Nuclear weapons are relatively cheap, but both spend money on the fabrication and development of this weaponry while knowing very well that the use of these weapons will destroy not only their enemy but also themselves. While the technical, financial, and strategic aspects of nuclear weapons are well beyond the current comprehension of psychiatrists, the peculiar Soviet-United States relationship of dependence on each other but also on a product that gives them so much power and threatens them with annihilation—merits psychiatric understanding.

Psychiatric contributions to the field of international relations are important but limited, and the judicious use, limitation of use, and possible abuse of psychiatric contributions have to be carefully observed. But we psychiatrists need to broaden our understanding of human relationships which exist under fierce and harsh realities.

The "togetherness" reflected in the ownership of the nuclear arsenal represents a burdensome tie between two powerful countries with different lifestyles, ideologies, and ethos. How much individuation is possible under these circumstances, and how much accentuation of separation and hostility is forced upon them because of their mortal tie? Psychiatrists can learn how unwilling partners in a relationship which they have created are tied to their product and through it, with each other. The splitting of mankind into bad and good guys is a luxury in which politicians can indulge, but not psychiatrists. We have the

25

responsibility to simultaneously see the good and the bad and to integrate them in our empathic understanding. This is an exercise in empathy far beyond our usual horizon. From it we can learn the limitations of our abilities for tolerance and understanding.

The balance of terror between the United States and the Soviet Union is a macabre dance performed on the world stage. The partners use that stage to enhance their perception of mutual distrust, not for direct interaction. They "externalize" their duel into spheres of influence or crisis spots, and use surrogate friends and foes. The overall U.S.–Soviet relationship, however, is ongoing; at times subtle, at times strident, but always, despite the dance, aimed and geared toward eliciting response. It represents a study in distancing and closeness, promises and unspoken threats, ambiguities and certainties, use and misuse of communication, alterations in patterns of relationship, and avoidance of contact because of an overwhelming, overriding constant awareness of each other.

The U.S.–Soviet relationship under the umbrella of nuclear weapons is based on mutual perceptions, subject to the impact of a harsh, awesome reality that is completely unimaginable and beyond our human dimension.

The existence, propagation, sophistication, and further development of nuclear weapons depend on the assumptions that antagonists have of each other about the intent or will to initiate conflict.[1] These antagonists are preoccupied only with "the points of conflict in various parts of the world that may escalate into violent disputes,"[2] or with the political or social changes that take place within their counterpart's arenas (the U.S. usually looking at the potential social changes in the U.S.S.R., the U.S.S.R. looking at electoral possibilities in the U.S.) As is common in conflicted relationships, they do not look into their own political and social changes that influence, or could or should influence, their perceptions. This preoccupation with a perceived enemy—who has a completely different ideology, political culture, social structure, past, and future aspirations—aggrandizes and distorts interactions. First of all, one is inclined to see something completely different through one's own prism which distorts; secondarily, preoccupation with another eclipses and

26

skews the perceptions of one's own realities. In his article on "The Global Military Balance," Paul H. Nitze stated:

> How does the Soviet Union look at this range of issues? A dozen or so of Washington's specialists in Soviet strategic thought and literature, participating in a discussion group in 1977, concurred in the following propositions. First, the Soviet leaders think that a nuclear war with the United States would result in a holocaust. Second, the Soviet leaders do not want a nuclear war with the United States. Third, the Soviet leaders increasingly regard a nuclear war as unthinkable. Fourth, the Soviet leaders believe the Soviet Union must be, if at all possible, in a position both to win and to survive a nuclear war with the United States if such a war, nevertheless, were to occur.[3]

We have little access to Soviet specialists' writings on American foreign policy that might state their assumption about U.S. intent, but we can shudder at the calculations that presumably are the basis for fabricating and perfecting this awesome weaponry. The most sophisticated technology, the efforts of the brightest technicians, the greatest financial contributions all combine to produce a preparedness based on assumptions about the intent of an aggrandized enemy. There is inadequate reality validation, no screening for self-deception, no awareness of the influence of technical developments, of interest groups, of reawakened historical hurts (and memories of such hurts) and of input in oneself and one's counterpart of personality factors. The examination of what the U.S. implants in its perception of the U.S.S.R., and of what the U.S.S.R. implants in its perceptions of the U.S. is avoided. Instead, there is preoccupation with other arenas: Sino-Soviet/ Sino-American relations, Eastern Europe, Yugoslavia, South Africa, the Middle East, European Common Market, Eurocommunism, NATO, Warsaw Pact, human rights, the other's economic capability, etc. The impact of these external relationships is extremely complex and continuously shifting. Each move is reacted upon, not only in accordance with what happened but in reaction to perception of motives.

Sino-Soviet and Sino-American relations have a mighty impact frequently leading to over-reaction; this is partially due to the immensity and complexity of suddenly having to comprehend China, which for its part has tremendous difficulty comprehending itself in its sudden convoluted changes. A quarter of the world's population has been ignored, misused, and then suddenly brought into the balancing act of the fierce Soviet–U.S. nuclear relationship. China has undergone sociopolitical convulsions that it has not yet absorbed, and it is under the raw impact of its "four modernizations": science, industry, defense and agriculture. But the most sudden change was the dethroning of Maoism with emphasis on agriculture, and the move instead toward rapid industrialization with the U.S. as a model. Soviet-U.S. perceptions have been profoundly altered and are constantly preoccupied with the impact of this gigantic, constantly changing China.

Eastern Europe and Yugoslavia have backgrounds that interpose themselves in the creation of conflict. Their histories, their nationalistic squabbles, their memories of how they have been treated by the West and the East, plus their geopolitical realities make them experts in permeating and perpetuating conflicted relationships. Recently, Africa has been dragged into the world of fierce conflict between the U.S. and the U.S.S.R., before it has had a chance to deal with its own bitter dilemmas. The Middle East, of course, has its own agenda.

This constant involvement of others increasingly veils the reading and perceptions of one's own direction and mood as well as reading the perceptions of one's counterpart. The perceptions the U.S. and U.S.S.R. have of each other are constantly being bombarded with input resulting in changing perceptions.

The sociocultural analysis of each other's political and cultural trends is all too often done by analysts who, beyond their training, have a special psychocultural affinity for the area. This affinity is often based on heritage, family ties, and the like. Their emotional interest makes the analysts avid readers and observers of all that is written and said about the area. This kind of subjectivity lends itself to distortions in perceptions and sometimes, to a certain degree, to evangelism and missionary zeal. Analysts with backgrounds and allegiances in Eastern Europe might perceive sociocultural trends through their Balkanized, nationalistic, unresolved allegiances, while analysts in the U.S.S.R., who have been steeped and immersed in American language and living styles, might view and describe the U.S. political culture through the prism of their indoctrination and through whatever made them become expert on the U.S.

There is nothing unusual about choosing a profession or area of interest because of or through one's emotional ties. Psychiatrists know that only too well. But we are trained to look within ourselves and to examine our motivations. Political analysts are not. They are usually offended by such an approach. They develop a profound attachment to their area of interest; that is what makes them experts. They do not look at their blind spots and prejudices. Thus, the analysts of the Soviet Union in the Middle East will frequently have unresolved emotional biases about the Soviet Union. Analysts in the United States of the Arab world are frequently intellectuals whose formative years of endeavor were spent in that part of the world, embracing its culture, language, ethos, and lifestyle. This permeates their writings, analyses, and political forecasts.

There is another theme which sets the tone of the U.S.-Soviet interaction. The United States has been used to unquestioning and unquestionable superstatus role. "The Kremlin's quest for full superpower status and consequent recognition that its interest must be considered in whatever regional arrangements are reached"[4] is dictated by nuclear developments mixed with historical aspirations. Indeed, this is what ties the Soviet-U.S. interaction so strongly to their nuclear arsenals. The United States wants the Soviet Union to dedicate itself more to the needs of its people with a "diminishing emphasis on defense."[5] The United States waits for a "constructive, conciliatory attitude of the Soviet elite."[6] But the Soviet elite knows that its superpower status and parity with the U.S. depends *only* on the possession of nuclear weapons. The old feelings of hurt, because Western man looked down on Eastern man until the U.S.S.R.'s nuclear arsenal no longer permitted such ignorance, are incentives to build up the arsenal even at the expense of the U.S.S.R. consumer.

Recommendations that the United States consider

unilateral disarmament as an incentive for disarmament of the U.S.S.R. has been proposed. This is utopian. The nuclear weapons cannot be dreamed away: they are a harsh, fierce, awesome reality of our times, and perhaps a necessity; they demand the most careful analyses, caution, examination, correction of perception, evaluation, and monitoring. The gruesome U.S.-Soviet interaction they create should be overseen by a standing *psychopolitical* commission. Several investigators have suggested that world tensions and fluctuations be monitored regularly and formally—almost as methodically as the weather—so that crises which might precipitate the hasty use of nuclear weapons could be anticipated and avoided. Such a system might help the public to recognize patterns of events and behavior of leaders and in turn aid in public scrutiny of the actions of government, especially the superpowers.

Our survival and the survival of our world could and must become a stronger, more realistic Soviet-U.S. tie than the awesome bond of nuclear weaponry. The shackled bond which nuclear weapons create between the superpowers makes these two giants immensely dependent on each other. Ambivalence around that dependency triggers off accentuated aggressive feelings towards each other. The anger is not consciously experienced but warded off through externalization. Not only is one's own aggression seen as that belonging to the opponent, but also a need to protect oneself more by a stronger and bigger nuclear arsenal. Consciously though one knows very well that the opponent will do the same. The discomfort of hostile dependency is increased with heightened ambivalence and aggression.

Partially the superpowers deal with this unconscious and conscious dilemma by offering themselves as the "protectors" of other "helpless" nations. The dependency on the superpowers of the surrogate antagonists increases the virulence of the international emotional climate. The surrogate antagonists resent their dependency on their superpowers ally and their inferior and helpless status in relationship to them. In order to avoid facing the sources of this anger, the dependent ally resolves the crisis by regressive maneuvers and increases his demands on his protector. The protector (the superpower) then places more missiles on his allies' terrain. That increases the "allies' vulnerability" and therefore dependency on the superpower and perpetuates the fierce, "macabre dance" between the superpowers.

The macabre bond between the U.S. and U.S.S.R. via nuclear weaponry can be considered the most perilous disease of mankind because of its potential impact. The "bond" psychologically breeds mistrust. Our planet's survival demands the development of some trust. The following psychological considerations would help develop some trust:

1) The two superpowers have to become more aware of the awesome reality of their partnership. This awareness demands recognizing by each of them that theirs is not a true aspiration for peace but a quest for supremacy under the disguise of peaceful intent.
2) Change of focus: Rather than continuously looking at the counterparts, motivation, aim, shortcomings, political and emotional climates and economic realities, the two superpowers have to gain a better understanding of their own social, economic, political, and psychological realities which breed mistrust.
3) Emphasis should be on asymmetry and differences between the two superpowers, rather than a tendency towards seeing the counterpart through the prism of one's own historical and present day realities.

If the U.S. would carefully analyze and understand the interaction between its historical strains and its present day reality and psychopolitical and emotional climate, it would be more in tune with its own needs and less subject to misunderstanding and misreading of Soviet intentions.

If the U.S.S.R. would carefully look at its historical strains from the 17th and 18th centuries and the interaction between these givens and its present ideology and motivation, it would be less inclined to read into the U.S.'s mood and motivation its own dilemmas.

The emotional climate in the U.S. changes abruptly every decade. The pendulum swings from simplistic '50s, ambiguous '60s, and conservative '70s, etc.[7] These abrupt swings are due to a reluctance by the U.S. to accept an inability not to solve everything. These swings produce

31

dizziness for a world who attempts to read U.S. intention, motivation, and direction. The U.S. cannot possibly understand the Soviet Union's burden and preoccupation with regime security and its multi-ethnicity burden as long as they judge it from the U.S. experience. Both superpowers would understand each other better and would tolerate each other's motivations if they would focus and gain a better understanding of their own realities and motivations.

4) Harsh, realistic evaluation of economic interests: There is a psychological tendency to avoid seeing the critical importance which economic realities have for one's counterpart when one badly needs them oneself. A hungry man will avoid seeing hunger in his opponent, but a hungry mother will suffer more from the hunger of her child than from her own. And here lies the severe dilemma which oil produces in the antagonistic, mistrusting relationship between the superpowers. In order for them to develop better confidence and trust, they need to understand, realize, and tolerate the critical importance that oil has: not only for themselves, but also for their allies, their counterpart and the counterpart's allies. But the superpowers cannot develop that understanding without some basic trust in each other.

The present relationship between the superpowers is one of mistrust. Beyond the strategic, political, historical, economic, and social realities there are also emotional tensions from the fierce shackles of the nuclear bond between them. This bond created for their "survival" is the one most likely to destroy them. They cannot extricate themselves from it, and it involves them in a macabre dance of fixation on each other which distorts their reality perceptions of themselves and their perceived enemies. They focus on each other's vulnerabilities which bind them to their own Achilles heel. It contaminates perceptions from the past with those of the present and distorts aspirations for the future. It decreases understanding about the counterpart's motivation and increases mistrust.

It is recommended that this pathological fixation on each other because of the awesome nuclear bond demands subtle, international, interdisciplinary intervention. Such intervention could be accomplished by a series of workshops dedicated specifically towards issues of trust versus mistrust. Emphasis would be placed not on who did what to whom but would focus on the awesome reality of the nuclear bond between the superpowers, on their preoccupation with each other which distracts and skews their views, not only about their counterpart but also obscures their realistic views of themselves and their abilities to change with a changing world.

References

1. Kirk G, Wessell NH (eds): The Soviet Threat: Myths and Realities. New York, The Academy of Political Science, 1978, p vii
2. *Ibid*
3. Nitze PH: The global military balance, in The Soviet Threat: Myths and Realities. p 5
4. Simes KK: Human rights and detente, in The Soviet Threat: Myths and Realities. p 145
5. *Ibid*
6. *Ibid*, p 146
7. Gelb L: Symposium on U.S.A.-U.S.S.R. Relationships. KCET, Channel 28, May 31, 1981

NUCLEAR WEAPONS AND SECRECY

Doyle I. Carson, M.D.

Secrecy has been an instrument of government policy from the beginning of the United States; all U.S. Presidents, including George Washington, have employed it to some degree, and it has been commonly accepted as essential to the military security of the nation. Generally, however, secrecy in the past was short-lived and related to specific, immediate military situations such as the departure time of troop ships, battle plans, etc. As a result, government secrecy was not ordinarily maintained beyond the time period during which a particular military threat existed. But in the nuclear age, secrecy, once invoked, has lingered. This has created a public tendency to expect and accept secrecy, certainly in government military operations and to some extent even in civilian aspects of life. Consequently there are a variety of questions that should be raised about the possible psychological effects of extensive secrecy on individuals and about ways in which pervasive secrecy affects the society at large.

Secrecy in the United States

Government secrecy has always presented a dilemma for the United States, a nation whose democratic processes can be most effective only when an informed public participates in them. The idea that military security can only be achieved by a policy of secrecy directly confronts the public's right to know and inhibits their capacity to know. Compounding this natural conflict between military secrecy and the principles of democratic openness has been the misuse of the concept of secrecy. The official power to hide information has at times permitted presidents and other government officials to utilize deception and outright dishonesty in order to achieve certain political goals.

There are numerous examples along these lines. President Andrew Jackson supported a brutal policy to remove Indians to west of the Mississippi but disguised this motive behind benevolent statements. In 1846, President James K. Polk dishonestly reported that Mexico had crossed the border of the United States and asked Congress to declare war, which it did. In recent times, secrecy regarding the Vietnam War and Watergate had political motivation well beyond national security interests.

Extensive classification systems for secrecy have developed within the Executive branch of government involving enormous numbers of people and material. These systems have often developed without Congressional approval or careful Congressional monitoring.

The use and abuse of secrecy for purposes of national defense and the national dilemma that results are not new phenomena, nor is the concomitant public distrust. What *is* new, though, is what we might call "chronic" secrecy, which has developed since World War II.

Secrecy in the Nuclear Age

Several factors converged in the development of this state of extensive chronic secrecy. First, there was the persistence of the wartime apparatus for secrecy. Secrecy was essential to the success of military efforts during World War II. Battle plans, espionage, counterespionage, weapons development, the D-Day invasion, and certainly the bombing of Hiroshima and Nagasaki were all enveloped in utmost secrecy. The mechanisms for accomplishing this were complex; they developed over many years, and they endured into the post–World War II era partly because of the difficulty inherent in dismantling such machinery once it is in place.

No sooner had World War II ended than began Cold War confrontations between the Western Allies and the Communist Bloc nations. China soon entered the Communist camp and international tension ran high; military preparedness became the order of the day in the United States and elsewhere, with accompanying secrecy of military plans and technology. Undercover operations became extensive throughout the world and the Central Intelligence Agency grew, all built on foundations laid during the war.

35

But it was the advent of nuclear technology which irrevocably altered the role of secrecy following World War II. The stakes of war became so high and the destructive power of nuclear weapons so awesome that secrecy itself became a weapon—the lid on national tendencies, which had been freely exerted in the past, to resolve conflicts by military action. Fear of nuclear technology in the hands of unfriendly governments augmented the emphasis on international secrecy.

Following World War II, there was also the development of new technology that could be used in "spying," which in turn provoked increasing degrees of secrecy to protect against the new technology—a cycle. Improved communication techniques were utilized in undercover operations. Private conversations were no longer inviolate no matter where they were held. Advances in photography have continued to be amazing. It has been predicted that orbiting satellites will eventually take pictures from space so sharp and precise that the license plate number on a car on earth will be discernible. The photograph will be developed in space and electronically transmitted to earth. Such technological advances perpetuate countermoves to keep sensitive information secret, and even the technological advances themselves are deemed sensitive information—another cycle. Thus, it would appear that since World War II, several different factors have acted to promote extensive lasting secrecy while much confusion has existed regarding its purpose. There has been general support for keeping vital military information secret but less agreement about what should be considered vital. In his work, *Nuclear Secrecy and International Policy,* Dr. Harold L. Nieberg outlined four different phases of America's policy of nuclear secrecy:

1. Manhattan District Project: during World War II, the intent was to develop nuclear weapons before the Germans and without their knowledge, and at the same time to prevent the development of these nuclear weapons by either allies or enemies of the U.S.
2. *1946–1953:* to prevent or delay development of nuclear weapons by Russia was sought.
3. *1953–1960:* the purpose of secrecy during this

phase was to prevent nations other than Russia from developing nuclear weapons.

4. *1960–On:* the secrecy during this phase remained about the same as previously but there was emphasis upon non-nuclear military options so that the U.S. was not relying entirely on nuclear force to resolve its international conflicts.[1]

As originally designed, the purpose of the policy of nuclear secrecy was to give the United States a monopoly over nuclear weapons and therefore a definite position of nuclear superiority over the rest of the world. This policy failed. Today, nuclear weapons are possessed by the Soviet Union, the United Kingdom, France, China, and India. Israel, South Africa, and Pakistan either have the bomb or are well on their way to making it. There are now no impenetrable secrets about how to build nuclear weapons. Several times in recent years, university students have looked into published literature on fission weapons and pieced together the necessary information to design an A-bomb; one report indicated that an A-bomb could be built for $1,900. Currently because nuclear secrecy is used to prevent others from designing an A-bomb, the policy appears to be more directed at terrorist groups, individuals, and underdeveloped nations. The success of this policy is questionable.

Secrecy and Nuclear War Strategy

Since the original purpose of nuclear secrecy was to prevent other nations from building nuclear weapons, and since that policy failed, the purpose and advisability of nuclear secrecy has been questioned. However, the value of nuclear secrecy is undergoing a temporary resurgence with a changing national nuclear strategy. In the past, the strategy of massive retaliation on the part of the United States and the Soviet Union has acted as a deterrent to nuclear war. Neither side would win with such "mutually assured destruction."

However, the United States and the Soviet Union are now developing policies that indicate a belief that one side could win a limited nuclear war. Improved weapons, missile technology, and extensive information about the location of each country's vulnerable national security positions (missile locations, communications centers, command centers, radar installations, troop locations, air fields, etc.) has shifted the strategy. There is a developing belief that one nation could attack first, cripple the other nation's nuclear capability, and achieve victory. Thus there is an emerging interest in developing more mobile nuclear attack weapons for defensive purposes. By continuously moving these weapons under the cloak of secrecy, a nation has a better chance of withstanding an initial nuclear attack. Accordingly, the purpose of nuclear secrecy has gradually shifted from preventing bomb design to hiding the location of the key military components necessary to deliver a nuclear attack such as the MX missile system and nuclear-warhead-equipped submarines.

Psychosocial Problems of Secrecy

While the utilization of secrecy is considered essential to the achievement of certain national security goals, the negative aspects of secrecy are not well understood. Does chronic secrecy affect individuals or governments in adverse ways? Most of what can be said is speculative, but some considerations are:

A) Support or enhancement of denial

The destructive potential of nuclear weapons is nearly incomprehensible. In the middle range of H-bombs, for example, the destructive power of each bomb is eighty times more powerful than the Hiroshima bomb. This is so overwhelming to comprehend and so personally threatening that any individual would appreciate being denied the facts and a policy of secrecy may enhance the natural tendency to deny nuclear threat. Thus, secrecy may aid the mental mechanism of denial. In so doing, secrecy may lessen anxiety but may also interfere with a realistic appraisal of nuclear dangers.

Furthermore, the ready use of denial in dealing with the specific threat of a nuclear holocaust may increase the general use of denial. In other words, is the use of denial directed toward issues, both individual and social, well beyond the nuclear sphere? Does this lead to a social system that fails to address certain problems; for example, family problems or job problems because of a widespread denial of their existence? After all, what problem, social or individual, can compare in scope to a widespread nuclear war? If the larger, more threatening issue is not to be openly acknowledged and confronted, why worry about lesser problems?

B) Outrage and distrust of government

When unpleasant events that have previously been kept secret become public, there tends to be outrage and distrust. The Three Mile Island incident was such an example, since there was widespread feeling that those who lived near the plant had not been warned adequately about the potential for plant accidents nor informed accurately about the accident once it occurred. The degree of mental stress associated with such discoveries of hidden government information is unclear. The persistence of extensive, chronic secrecy impairs accurate perception of governmental functioning. Facts are withheld that might alter individual and collective attitudes toward the government officials in power. On the one hand, there are those who tend to have an abiding faith in government and will accept secrecy as necessary and in the national interest. Secrecy in itself seems to enhance positive feelings toward government in such individuals. If unpleasant and surprising information is then released by the government, there is a sense of betrayal, breach of trust, and disappointment.

On the other hand, there are those who are disposed to mistrust the secrecy establishment and who have developed a distrust of government which may persist despite all efforts to allay suspicion. The popularity of spy thriller books and movies since World War II may, in part, be related to widespread public distrust of government and, in some cases, may reflect common fantasies.

C) Impaired perception of potential enemy

When governments hide their military strengths, the potential for overestimating or underestimating one another's military capacity and power exists. There are those who argue that this degree of uncertainty may, in fact, increase the risk of war rather than diminish it by precipitating ill-conceived military actions.

D) Impairment of democratic process

An essential feature in a democratic government is an informed public. Secrecy thwarts this process. In *The Politics of Lying*, David Wise wrote, "The consent of the governed is basic to American democracy. If the governed are misled, if they are not told the truth, or if through official secrecy and deception they lack information on which to base intelligent decisions, the system may go on—but not as a democracy."[2]

What price is paid by a society in the form of frustration, stress, and tension arising from this continuing conflict between secrecy and openness, since both are deemed essential to the highly valued goals of the society—military security and functioning democracy?

E) Tendency for secrecy apparatus to persist and grow

Once an extensive secrecy apparatus is developed within government, as we have discussed, it becomes difficult to alter. Like many large bureaucracies, it seems to develop a life of its own. A widespread government system of secrecy is not well monitored because of the very nature of secrecy. In time, increasing numbers of government documents become classified as secret and the secrecy apparatus grows. A common complaint of government officials who work with classified material is that the material does not seem to require such classification. In fact, the entire system of clearance and classification seems to increase the true power of those who hold the secrets, enhance their image as powerful people in the eyes of those who don't hold the secrets, and bestow a sense of power on those who by design or accident discover secrets. Thus the secrecy hierarchy may nourish itself on prestige—a quality sought by government officials, the media, and the public alike. Undoubtedly, these and other psychological factors play some role in the persistence of secrecy.

Regardless of the problems it presents, secrecy is integral to U.S. policy and will continue to be used extensively as long as perceived external military threats exist.

Secrecy will be especially extensive in terms of nuclear developments. Consequently, questions should be raised continually about the potential negative effects of chronic secrecy both on individuals and the society. A better understanding of the dynamic of secrecy would appear both pragmatic and wise.

References

1. Nieburg H: Nuclear Secrecy and International Policy. Washington DC, Public Affairs, 1964
2. Wise D: The Politics of Lying. New York, Random House, 1973

THREE MILE ISLAND: PSYCHOLOGICAL EFFECTS OF A NUCLEAR ACCIDENT AND MASS MEDIA COVERAGE

Michael Mufson, M.D.

Since the 1979 accident at Three Mile Island, a nuclear power plant near Harrisburg, Pennsylvania, and the concomitant publicity, people around the world have become more aware than ever of nuclear power plants and their potential danger. The majority of people report that the media is an important, if not the major, source of their information about nuclear advances.[1]

The extensive press coverage of Three Mile Island presented an opportunity to observe the psychological impact of the accident on the residents of the area surrounding the plant, as described by them and by reporters. It also provided an unprecedented opportunity to learn how the media coverage reflected, and in part established, the psychological climate on this issue.

It is important to review the details and tone of the reporting on Three Mile Island in order to obtain a sense of how the information given to the public evolved over the week of the accident. To do this we examined coverage in the *New York Times* and *Time* magazine, which we felt, on balance, to be representative, ongoing coverage.

The first report in the *New York Times* was on March 29, 1979, a front-page story entitled "Radiation Released in Accident at Nuclear Plant in Pennsylvania." This article, published approximately 12 hours after the "event," reported that the Nuclear Regulatory Commission (NRC) had "still not determined the full extent of the radiation danger." More important, however, was the report that "dispute began immediately" over the details of the accident and the "unexplained" cutoff of coolant. It described Metropolitan Edison's "reassuring" response to the public: "This is not a China Syndrome . . . only a few rods melted through."[2]

On March 30, articles on page one of the *New York*

Times were entitled "Atomic Plant Is Still Emitting Radioactivity" and "Nuclear Accident Is Laid to Failure of Several Safety Systems." Of interest in these reports were assurances that there was "no reason to feel public health was affected" and that the "system" had been brought under control. Instead of a few rods melting down, the figure quoted now was "108–360";[3] the question of human error was dismissed, and the accident was attributed to the failure of "two pumps and a valve."[4] In these reports, however, was the first sense of questioning about the safety of the released radioactivity. Harvard's Dr. George Wald was quoted as stating, "any dose is unsafe because there is no lower threshold for radiation."[5]

On March 31, there was a major shift in emphasis from technical details of the accident with illustrated diagrams of nuclear reactors[6] to front-page photos of school children and pregnant women leaving the area. The lead articles were now entitled "U.S. Aides See a Risk of Meltdown at Pennsylvania Nuclear Plant; More Radioactive Gas is Released"; "Children and Pregnant Women Near Plant Leave"; "Within Sight of Stricken Plant, A Town's Main Street is Empty"; and "An Unauthorized Alarm Brings on New Tension in Anxious Harrisburg." The shift to concern with the population rather than the plant was now obvious. In addition, the confusion of the situation became apparent with reports of the contradictory details released and Governor Thornburgh's "frustration" over recurring conflicting reports, "It is very difficult to pin these facts down. Our responsibility is to protect the citizens of central Pennsylvania."[7] The NRC now reported that *9,000 fuel rods may have been damaged* and described the onset of a "gas bubble" in the reactor. One official stated, "We are in a position not comparable to previous conditions,"[8] when referring to the new bubble. A meltdown had become a real possibility. Problems were described as "far worse," and evacuation of individuals "particularly susceptible" to the effects of radiation was begun.[9]

The psychological state of Harrisburg was clearly portrayed with pictures of empty streets and references to people's "fright" and their response to this fear with humor. People began to describe living near the plant as "like living with a rattlesnake" and referred to the accident as the "unthinkable."[10]

On April 1, there were four pages of coverage, including such articles as "A Calm Returns to Middletown" and "Officials Say Nuclear Plant Cooler but in Crisis." Evacuated elderly members of the community were pictured on page one, and continued concern was expressed for preschoolers and pregnant women. The scenario was described as a nightmare. People were stating, "I can't believe this is happening, what can we do?" Some began describing themselves as "survivors" and "victims."[11] The nuclear industry and nuclear power in general began to be seriously questioned well beyond the Harrisburg area.[12]

Interestingly, in the midst of the controversy, the Sunday *New York Times Magazine* published a lead article on "Challenging the Myths of National Security." This analysis identified four myths: the myth of defense, the myth of deterrence, the myth of military power, and the myth of an arms economy. The article seriously challenged the proliferation of nuclear advances as a means of assuring national defense and made specific references to the "precarious peace" and "risky margin of error" in a "violent, unstable world." It went on to say that "myths which brought comfort in the past now threaten to destroy us."[13] It was as if the article had been written about nuclear power plants.

These themes were not unique to the reporting in the *New York Times*. The April 9th cover of *Time* magazine showed dusk over the twin towers of Three Mile Island and read, "A Nuclear Nightmare." The articles emphasized that a "nuclear catastrophe is possible" and that the "failsafe gadgets of nuclear technology are as fallible as the men who built them." The *Time* coverage also captured the language of Metropolitan Edison and the NRC over the week, referring to the "event" as a "normal aberration" and "routine mechanical failure" and later, when the situation was more complicated: "We didn't injure anybody. We didn't kill a single soul," and finally, "We are in a situation that is not a situation we have ever been in before." The reports also captured the responses of the Harrisburg residents, "I don't know what to believe, what to do, so I guess the best thing is to go. It's better than doing nothing. I just believed what the company said. Now I don't." And in the terms of Senator Majority Leader Robert Byrd, "There's going to be a great difficulty on the part of American people to feel absolutely reassured about nuclear power."[14]

On April 16, *Time*'s follow-up article was "Now Comes the Fallout," and the new themes that "gone was confidence" and a need for "reappraisal and caution" in that the "unthinkable had come to happen."[15]

The reporting pointed out that the American people had had an "incredibly intensive education course." David Rosenbaum, physicist, was quoted as saying, "The public has been deluded into thinking that if all scientists just buckle down they can figure it all out. That's not true." Alluding to this issue, Senator Lowell Weicker of Connecticut asked the NRC, "Who's in control of a situation like this?"

Emphasizing the traumatic nature of the previous two weeks, *Time* noted that people in Harrisburg were back from the "brink" and referred to them as Three Mile Island "survivors," reinforcing the labeling of the population. The prospect of ongoing anxiety for the "survivors" was summarized in a resident's comment "Those four cooling towers will never look so innocent again."[15]

The accident of Three Mile Island can be examined in the context of the variety of stresses to which the population had to respond and their psychological responses to these stresses.

In terms of acute stress, if one analyzes the ongoing press coverage, it is apparent that the population was exposed to a rapid succession of circumstances that were overwhelming in character and incomprehensible at times due to the complexity of the technology involved. Also, this already complex information reached the population in a new, unfamiliar language featuring such terms as "stable shutdown," "normal aberration," "event," and others.

Then, while the population was trying to assimilate this jargon, the jargon changed as numerous contradictory reports were released. The population's ability to trust official reports and messages was constantly undermined, and thus its capacity to be reassured diminished.

As the days passed, the stress increased as it became clear that with the seemingly irresolvable development of the "bubble," technology and experts were fallible and possibly to blame. By the middle of the crisis people were exposed to the imagery of nightmares and the uncertainty of "refugee" status accompanied by fear. They experienced the feeling of a need to flee—and the helplessness which accompanies the sense that life is out of control. As the crisis was resolved, the population faced the job of integrating the experience.

Until more detailed interviews of the Harrisburg population are done, the characteristics unique to their psychological response will not be known. We do, however, have knowledge of studies of people under stress and survivors of other disasters that allow us to advance some hypotheses around the psychological impact of the Three Mile Island accident. In addition, the 1964 GAP report, Psychiatric Aspects of the Prevention of Nuclear War, presented an overview of the psychological functions involved in how individuals and groups respond to nuclear arms, which is in part applicable to Three Mile Island. Finally, our Task Force has obtained preliminary questionnaires from people in the Harrisburg environs giving support to the hypothesis that their responses are similar to those of other "survivors."

The 1964 GAP report cited fear as an adaptive response motivating the individual to avoid danger and survive.[16] The report detailed the "primitivizing" effects of fear and subsequent distortion in people's fantasies and internal experience of a situation. Excessive fear destroys the capacity for adaptive discrimination, shortens the time perspective at hand, leads the individual to act precipitously, and, in extreme circumstances, leads to functional paralysis.

The GAP report also noted how patterns of response to danger include denial (i.e., various degrees of non-perception, non-recognition, non-understanding, or non-acceptance of certain realities in order to cope with otherwise unacceptable intrapsychic conflicts, feelings or memories) and isolation of affect, (i.e. separation of the affect from associated thought content).[17]

Of even more interest is the GAP description of the inadequacy of language in the nuclear context to describe new phenomena, and how this inadequacy leads to the failure of emotional comprehension of an event that has never been experienced or is of extraordinary magnitude. This reminds one of the Harrisburg population's task of assimilating an occurrence regarded as the "unthinkable." Finally the report described the anxiety provoked by having the individual's myth of personal invulnerability challenged.[18]

The GAP report described the effect of nuclear fears on "dehumanizing" an individual and how this leads to increased emotional distance from others, a diminished sense of personal responsibility for the consequences of one's actions, and feelings of personal helplessness.[19] The data around the Three Mile Island accident support the notion that all of these psychological factors can be found in the response of the population in Harrisburg.

The general fear of the population can best be summed up in Governor Thornburgh's statement, "Not all the promotion in the world can erase the memories of central Pennsylvania as the place where the worst fear of modern man almost came to pass."

The primitivizing effect of fear was obvious in the government's awareness of the need to reassure the population that there was no reason to panic, while simultaneously a sense of urgency was apparent in the hasty evacuation plans that were instituted.

Preparation for evacuation was seen as necessary immediately, before more serious developments occurred, and precautions had to be taken in what certainly appeared to be the "shortened time perspective" resulting from the fear of immediate danger from the plant. It is important to note that the fear elicited by the Three Mile Island accident was based on a combination of intangible and unknown "conditions" and a reality-based sense of imminent danger. The reality included the belief in the possibility of exposure to massive radiation and the subsequent risks to children, pregnant women, and the general population; the unknown element was the possible scenario of a meltdown.

This unique blend of known and unknown fear emphasizes the importance of exploring the fantasies of the inhabitants of the area surrounding Three Mile Island. The behavioral reactions in the face of an external threat reflect the meaning of the confronting stimulus, the accuracy of one's perceptions about it, one's previous experience in similar situations, and the degree of distortion by fantasies.[20] Given the unprecedented nature of the Three Mile Island accident, the degree of distortion via fantasy must have been great. It should be stressed that the symbolic meaning of an event can be more threatening than the event itself. Given the imagery described by the Three Mile Island population—"nightmares," "radiation," "living with a rattlesnake"—one suspects the internal experience to be fraught with death imagery, lingering anxiety, and feelings of helplessness.

In addition to fear, it is clear that people at Three Mile Island responded with denial: "I can't believe this is happening." Denial on the part of officials of Metropolitan Edison and the NRC also explains some of the contradictory reports and indeed may have helped these officials cope with their own anxieties, which they could not publicly express.

But although denial helps alleviate anxiety, the clear threat to the individual's myth of invulnerability stripped people of this defense for the most part in the Three Mile Island event. Indeed, the *New York Times Magazine* article on national security discussed the tendency of the nation as a whole to believe itself invulnerable, a belief that is no longer founded in reality.

Another aspect of the Three Mile Island crisis was the lack of warning; its sudden yet imposing nature. Robert Lifton discussed the significance of suddenness in his analysis of the Buffalo Creek disaster, which occurred in West Virginia in February 1972. In this incident, a dam burst because a company dumped excessive amounts of coal waste into the creek. The resultant flood of heavy black water left 5,000 homeless and killed 125. Lifton found that two months after the disaster, survivors were still preoccupied with the abrupt transition from normalcy. They related that their inability to understand or accept what happened was in part due to the suddenness with which it occurred. The sense was that in this type of event, the ego had no time to prepare its defenses.[21] It appears that the suddenness and terror of a disaster intensify both its immediate and long-range effects on the person.

Horowitz, in writing on stress response syndromes, found that traumatic events are responded to with ideational denial and emotional numbing.[22] This is similar to the psychic numbing Lifton described in his analysis of survivors. Horowitz also found a pattern to the progress of phases of stress response. With a sudden, unanticipated event, he found emotional reactions such as "crying out" or "stunned uncomprehension." After these first emotional reactions, he described periods of denial and numbing followed by an oscillating period in which there are episodes of intrusive ideas or images, attacks of emotion, or compulsive behaviors alternating with continued denial, numbing, and other indications of efforts to ward off the implications of the new information. This is followed by a final phase of less intrusive thoughts and less uncontrolled attacks of emotion with greater recognition, conceptualization, stability of mood, and acceptance of the meanings of the event.

The question one must raise with a nuclear accident revolves around the potential ongoing nature of the stress, due to the fear that exposure to radiation has long term effects and, that may only be known years down the road. Will this extend the initial phases of the response, inhibiting a psychic resolution and prolonging the disequilibrium of stages one and two? Horowitz also described the activation of themes whereby the individual sees his self being both victimized and damaged.[23] Both feelings were expressed in our questionnaires.

A detailed study of this survivor state has been done by Lifton in his analysis of the survivors of the Buffalo Creek experience.[24] He described the pervasive emotional response of psychic numbing or partial emotional desensitization, the most universal response to disaster, which enables the survivors to deal with their anxiety over their encounter with death and disaster. The forms of this may be apathy, withdrawal, depression, or constriction of living. Numbing serves to protect the individual and allow him not to deal with the consequences of the disaster.

In the Three Mile Island accident, however, as discussed earlier, one wonders how effective this mechanism was, given the daily barrage of media details. Each day of the crisis people were confronted with the potential dangers of nuclear technology. Whereas prior to this event psychic numbing may have served to distance the individual from the effects of nuclear technology, with Three Mile Island we entered a new era in which individuals could be exposed daily to an intense encounter with the idea of a nuclear accident. This raises the question of what the intrapsychic consequences will be for such individuals. Lawrence Langer, in his book *The Age of Atrocity*, pointed out how the modern age challenges the individual to be in touch with the intolerable and to remain psychologically whole.[25] This indeed summarizes the difficulty of those who lived near Three Mile Island.

Robert Lifton also documented the survivor mission that arises from survivor states. There is now emerging in the survivors of Three Mile Island an awareness of the possibility that they and their children may have been exposed to dangerous levels of radiation. Living with this awareness may stimulate guilt. One person interviewed by the Task Force stated, "I am hesitant to have children after the Three Mile Island accident. Suppose my husband and I develop cancer because of the accident and ongoing exposure to radiation? Who will continue to bring up our children?" There is also a sense of mission to relieve this guilt, "I will not be forced from my home. I will fight nuclear energy first."

In short, the survivor begins to see himself as a victim with damage to his psychological self, his body, his belief of invulnerability, and his innocence. He begins to question the relationship of the disaster to the irresponsibility of other human beings. In Buffalo Creek, the people quickly recognized that the disaster was caused by others, and the survivors expressed their sense of profound humiliation at the low value those others appeared to place upon the survivors' lives. At Three Mile Island this reaction can be discerned in the many inquiring comments made about trust in the representatives of the government and the nuclear industry. People began to see all experts as fallible and wonder about the values of the utility spokespersons. As one Three Mile Island "survivor" answered on the Task Force questionnaire, "I'm beginning to question the trust I had in the government policy. The government and utilities are making decisions for the people that they have no moral right to make."

Lifton also related that certain individuals at Buffalo

Creek felt their humanity violated and unrecognized. They internalized that diminished sense of self in ways that impaired their capacity for recovery or even hope.[26] This recalls the maladaptive defense of self-directed dehumanization described in the GAP report, whereby the individual diminishes his capacity to feel and act like a human being.[27]

We are beginning to see survivors of Three Mile Island expressing this damaged sense of self. Recall the statement, "Suppose my husband and I develop cancer. . . . Who will bring up our children?" Indeed the concern expressed by this individual about her own self and her children's future leads to a final issue that must be considered in dealing with the psychological impact of the Three Mile Island accident in particular and nuclear power in general.

Erikson described the concept of generativity as a person's concern for establishing and guiding the next generation. He felt that a person who is to gain a sense of ego integrity, order, and meaning in his life will possess this generativity and pass it on to and care for the next generation. If this is not accomplished, the individual is left with despair and a sense of disgust, the feeling that time is short, and no vision of life.[28]

Reviewing our questionnaires and the responses of people at Three Mile Island, there certainly is the sense of interrupted generativity. The Pennsylvania respondents show a common concern with future generations, their children, and their genetic future. They communicate a depressed feeling about this future, anger arising from a sense of helplessness, and a sense of victimization. Many respondents report a feeling of life being shortened, a sense of life imbued with urgency, and a sense of danger. As one responded, "Thermonuclear advances contribute a great deal to my sense of powerlessness and make me somewhat more autistic and less global in my concerns."

One person felt that thermonuclear advances "makes people improve their security by living for the present as opposed to delaying satisfaction. It is contributing to a general decline in values, morals, and principles for living which previously gave life meaning."

These are serious concerns with which we all must struggle as the nuclear age advances, but they also illustrate the fact that people are reacting to these advances by questioning the traditional transfer of values and security to the next generation. There is a possibility that this will pose a real threat to the trust and faith the next generation possesses, leading to a generation with a less creative vision of life and a more narcissistic preoccupation than we have traditionally seen. This possibility is clearly described by Langer, who emphasized that artists in this nuclear age have begun to be less concerned with creating a future than fighting for the present: "Living in times of catastrophe shifts the rhythm of our imaginative efforts from creating the future—the challenge of our ancestors—to fighting a rearguard action against forces which menace us with annihilation. . . ."[29] He continued, "to embrace the possibility of death is to admit the possibility of inappropriate life, of a precarious existence which may be snuffed out without warning, leaving the survivors oblivious to any discernible relationship between cause and effect. For the imagination distilled in the crucible of such perception, the frontiers of the self shrink and survival requires that self to consider . . . not what men live by, but what men die by."[30]

On reviewing the mass media coverage and responses of the people in the proximity of Three Mile Island, it is clear that the accident had significant psychological impact. Inhabitants quickly have begun viewing themselves as survivors and expressing a damaged sense of self. There is an expression of being victimized at the hands of modern technology and the human beings behind that technology. This leads to a questioning and mistrust of traditional institutions once seen as infallible and now seen as agents of potential disaster.

An anxiety of damage to the individual self was experienced by the survivors of Three Mile Island, and moreover an ongoing anxiety is expressed over the meaning of the accident in relation to the biological future of their children. Although the estimates did not indicate a dangerous exposure to radiation, the emotional responses people have expressed indicate their fears and fantasies have not been alleviated by scientific explanations.

It does not appear that traditional defenses such as denial or emotional numbing were successful in defending against the fear and anxiety raised by the accident at Three Mile Island. It will be a major task of the survivors of this experience to integrate this experience and continue to live under the shadows of the towers of Three Mile Island. Already individuals are responding in a "survivor mission" way, combatting nuclear developments and expressing feelings of guilt about having endangered themselves and possible future generations.

It is clear that as nuclear developments spread more people will be exposed to similar potential dangers. We will have to be prepared to understand their responses and help them remain "psychologically whole" in dealing with their futures and those of their children.

References

1. Data from the Task Force questionnaire
2. Janson D: Radiation is released in accident at nuclear plant in Pennsylvania. New York Times, March 29, 1979
3. Lyons R: Atomic plant is still emitting radioactivity. New York Times, March 30, 1979
4. *Ibid*
5. *Ibid*
6. Burnham D: Nuclear accident is laid to failure of several safety systems at plant. New York Times, March 31, 1979
7. Franklin B: An authorized alarm brings on new tension in anxious Harrisburg. New York Times, March 31, 1979
8. Burnham D: U.S. agency sees a risk of fuel melting. New York Times, March 31, 1979
9. Lyons R: U.S. aides see a risk of meltdown at Pennsylvania plant; more radioactive gas is released. New York Times, March 31, 1979
10. Ayres D: Within sight of stricken plant, a town's main street is empty. New York Times, March 31, 1979
11. Ayres D: A calm returns to Middletown, but some continue to lie low. New York Times, April 1, 1979
12. Severo D: Debate about safety of nuclear plants intensifies in the tristate region. New York Times, April 1, 1979
13. Barnet R: Challenging the myths of national security. New York Times Magazine, April 1, 1979
14. Time, April 9, 1979, pp 8-20
15. Time, April 16, 1979, pp 22-24
16. Group for the Advancement of Psychiatry: Psychiatric Aspects of Nuclear War, Report 57. New York, 1964, p 237
17. *Ibid*, pp 237-244
18. *Ibid*, p 243
19. *Ibid*, pp 245-256
20. *Ibid*, pp 237-238
21. Lifton RJ, Olsen E: The human meaning of total disaster: the Buffalo Creek experience. Psychiatry 3:1-9, 1976

22. Horowitz M: Stress response syndromes. Arch Gen Psychiatry 31:768-770, 1979
23. *Ibid*, p 770
24. Lifton RJ, Olsen E: *op cit*, p 8
25. Langer L: The Age of Atrocity. Boston, Beacon Press, 1978, p xii
26. Lifton RJ, Olsen E: *op cit*
27. Group for the Advancement of Psychiatry: *op cit*, p 247
28. Erikson EH: Childhood and Society. New York, WW Norton, 1950, pp 266-268
29. Langer L: *op cit*, p xiii
30. *Ibid*, p 2

PSYCHOSOCIAL ASPECTS OF NUCLEAR POWER: A REVIEW OF THE INTERNATIONAL LITERATURE

Michael Mufson, M.D.

The nuclear accident at Three Mile Island brought the debate over nuclear power to the forefront of American consciousness. This debate has been raging, however, throughout Europe and in many other countries during the past ten years. A review of the issues raised in these countries is presented below to illustrate the common psychological responses and themes arising in the consciousness of people around the world.

Perhaps the most intensive debate over nuclear power took place in Austria from October 1976 to November 1978. This debate most clearly demonstrated the themes found in many countries but was unique in the public debate that was staged for two years. Austria had no nuclear plants in operation in 1976 and a scheduled referendum was held in 1978 to determine if the one reactor "Zwetendorf," ready for completion, should be put into operation.

Prior to the referendum, the government staged a national information campaign from October 1976 to July 1978 covering the economic, sociologic, and political questions surrounding nuclear energy. The campaign was intended to supply adequate, unbiased information to the public in addition to providing material to the Parliament for future decisions on nuclear energy. During the first phase of the campaign, teams of experts comprised of both promoters and critics of nuclear energy debated issues in public and private forums and produced exhaustive reports. In the second phase, these reports were discussed in a series of symposia by representatives of different Austrian viewpoints on nuclear energy.[1]

The debates quickly became emotionally charged. In Linz in October 1976, during only the second public forum, chaos reigned; the reaction of the audience was so negative that the speakers had to leave the rostrum. By the tenth forum, it was necessary to cancel the scheduled debate because of an announcement of a large-scale anti-nuclear demonstration. As a result of the tumult surrounding the public information campaign, a second round of meetings of representatives from science, administration, and industry was held to discuss the pros and cons of nuclear energy. These were closed to the public and press.[2]

The nature of these public protests helps us understand the anxieties and concerns expressed by the Austrian people, which resulted in the ultimate rejection of the nuclear plant with a "no" vote on the referendum. The question of waste disposal raised perhaps the most opposition. The national government was met with vigorous local opposition to plans for disposal of waste inside Austria—in one province, three thousand farmers demonstrated against disposal near their land—and by July 1977 the government considered radioactive waste disposal issue the key problem. As such in October of that year the Austrian government was negotiating with Iran for storage of waste there, and in June 1978 negotiations began with Egypt to investigate storage sites in that country.

Of special interest was the opposition by the Austrian People's Party, which favored nuclear power in principle but based their opposition on the belief that safety considerations were not fulfilled. They focused on the need for continuous and assured control of "maximum permissible" doses of radiation in the area around the reactor, the lack of plans for nuclear waste disposal, and the lack of regional and supraregional emergency plans in case of a nuclear accident (Vienna is 40 kilometers from the site of the reactor) as the crucial matters not yet resolved.[3] This cautious position was taken even though two pronuclear organizations (The Association of Austrian Industrialists and The Austrian Economic Federation) were strong supporters of the Austrian People's Party.

The pronuclear position was that all safety requirements would be fulfilled and that opponents had not produced any evidence which showed the plant to be dangerous or uneconomic. In September 1978, polls showed that 56 percent of the Austrian people were in favor of the plant and 28 percent were opposed.

But on November 5, 1978, the Austrian people voted 50.4 percent to 49.53 percent to not put the nuclear plant into operation (64 percent of the electorate voted). In addition to the safety issues reviewed, the main concerns in the outcome were as follows.

Geologists raised questions about the location of the plant in an area vulnerable to earthquakes and suggested that an accident could contaminate the water supply to Vienna. Many opponents raised the spectre of radioactive contamination to the human environment, focusing on the effect on children, and anxieties surfaced about the possibility of children being exposed to long-term dangers of waste storage. As one group put it, "It is a political, ethical decision on the moral weight of prosperity—advantages for now on the one hand and the possible inevitable burden of health, economic, and social nature for many generations on the other hand."[4] Fears of terrorist activity emerged as a more "real" possibility as the months of debate continued. Finally the safety of the plant itself was called into question.[5]

It is important to note that in Austria the issues raised were covered in a balanced fashion by the press. In the months prior to the referendum, a review of the press coverage revealed articles presented both points of view. In September 1978, of 83 articles, 49 provided both sides of the debate, 14 were considered pronuclear, and 20 antinuclear. In November, 49 articles appeared; 28 were seen as balanced, 17 pronuclear, and four antinuclear.[6]

The vote on the nuclear referendum in Austria was complicated by internal political struggles. The antinuclear vote was seen by some analysts as gaining more plurality because potentially pronuclear voters abstained as protests against the ruling Chancellor. Our purpose here, however, is to focus on the nature of the debate and to compare it to other countries to obtain an overview of common psychosocial responses to nuclear power plant development.

Many of the concerns expressed in Austria are paramount in West Germany as well. In the upcoming years West Germany is scheduled to build at least 40 nuclear power plants, and consequently the same issues are high-lighted. What is termed the "atomic fight" in West Germany contrasts the idea of "securing work places" with that of "securing life and future."[7]

An analysis of public anxieties in Italy reveals again major issues surrounding waste disposal and safety of the reactor. An active information campaign was proposed to relieve such anxieties.[8] In England, too, public anxiety revolves around "acceptable limits of radiation, the worst conceivable accident and disposal of radioactive waste."[9]

The debate in Japan is similar. An overview article published in 1978 on the nuclear controversy there analyzed 20 monthly and weekly magazines (about 400 articles) and 86 newspapers (60,000 news items) from 1972 to 1975. The content clearly reflected a public preoccupation with the safety aspects of the nuclear power controversy.[10]

A year earlier, specific issues focusing on the sites for nuclear plants and the apprehensions of local inhabitants had been analyzed. Fears centered on the handling of radioactive wastes and "power generating techniques which do not plant roots in society."[11] The former issue can be seen as reflecting the individual's anxiety on the personal level, and this latter issue reflects deep concern by the Japanese that nuclear technology is an exclusively modern phenomenon, having no connection to or potential for establishing continuity with traditional structures of Japanese society.

Another Japanese review identified the major public acceptance problem as an outgrowth of the fear of re-processing plants; plants which recover reusable radioactive material. In these plants, highly radioactive material must be handled and almost perfect containment maintained to protect the public. Anxieties were seen to reflect fears of release of radioactive materials in normal and abnormal operations of the plants, disposal of wastes with high level radioactivity, the effects of radioisotopes on the environment, physical protection for the plant, and radiation exposure to the people operating the plant. In addition, this study pointed out how people were beginning to perceive atomic power as the symbol of "huge scale power"[12] that is possibly indifferent to the individual's needs and anxieties.

In Japan, of course, concerns over nuclear power plants are complicated by the special national sentiment arising from the atomic bombings of Hiroshima and Nagasaki and the suffering of Japanese fishermen resulting from the radioactive debris of the nuclear test explosion at Bikini Atoll. These experiences are now acutely juxtaposed against the need for nuclear power to solve Japan's severe energy problems. The Japanese, sensing that they are already "survivors" of nuclear destruction, thus find themselves struggling for answers. This is reflected in a public opinion poll from 1975 in which 48 percent of the people expressed fears of atomic energy but 70 percent took the need for granted and said that Japan had no choice but to depend on nuclear power.[13]

In discussing this poll, the authors suggested that while cities may benefit from the electricity generated by power plants, site areas will "endure the psychological pressures arising from the fear of radioactive contamination and environmental disruption."[14] They pointed out how Japan is a culture with a long tradition in which man and nature peacefully coexist. The authors noted that the necessity in Japan is to ensure that "nuclear power is developed in such a way that the harmony of nature and harmony with the people will be returned."[15]

We can begin to see clearly that nuclear developments in Japanese culture transcend the individual's anxieties about his own safety. The values of an entire culture are challenged, raising concerns not only of practical risks and benefits but also raising questions about the future character of life and society.

In this vein it will be useful to turn to a series of reports published by the International Atomic Energy Agency (IAEA) and the International Institute for Applied Systems Analysis which examine the factors influencing public beliefs about nuclear power and its risks.

In the study, The Perception of Technological Risks: A Psychological Perspective, Professor H. J. Otway suggested that the term "risk perception" was "coined by technologists as a result of the observation that public reactions to new technologies often seemed 'out of proportion' to the estimated levels of risk when they were compared to the (accepted) risks of daily life." Otway challenged the model of human behavior implied by the

concept of risk perception, which claims that: ". . . behaviors which reflect opposition to a technology *are*
determined by (perhaps inaccurate) perceptions of its
risks . . . that perceptions of risks should be determined
by 'objective' risk data and should be amenable to change
through rational forces of argument, if people could be
provided with technical facts."[16]

Using nuclear power as an example, Otway persuasively showed how perceptions of risk are determined by
multiple factors combining technical, psychological, and
social factors. He showed how comparisons of different
types of risks lack meaning, since each risk is characterized by many variables other than its statistical expectation. He referred, for example, to a concept termed "dread
risk," or an "instinctive, unexplained fear" of a technology and how this psychological factor plays a significant role in risk perception of nuclear advances.[17]

Otway also explained how technical information can
seldom be verified by one's own senses and thus does not
necessarily play a dominant role in the formation or
change of public attitudes on technical issues. He concluded that technical safety studies undertaken with the
idea of providing hard facts to influence public opinion
may thus have little effect on public attitudes.[18]

In another study of public acceptance of nuclear energy in Austria, Otway found four underlying dimensions
of public beliefs about that source of energy. These included psychologic risks, economic/technical benefits,
sociopolitical implications, and environmental/physical
risks. Psychologic risks expressed by people in this
sample revolved around fears that nuclear power would
expose an individual to risks they could not control.[19] In a
subsequent report comparing public beliefs about five
different energy systems (nuclear, solar, hydro, coal,
and oil), Otway found attitudes polarized only in the case
of nuclear energy and that only nuclear energy was
associated with psychologic and physical risks.

Otway also examined the accuracy of policymakers'
perceptions of the beliefs and attitudes of public groups
with respect to nuclear power. He found that the difference in overall attitudes between policy makers and the
public was primarily that for the public, psychological
risks were strongly associated with the case of nuclear

energy while environmental risks (pollution, production of noxious waste) made only a minimal positive contribution toward their attitude. He went on to note that policymakers' perceptions were diminished by their failure to recognize the extent to which issues of psychological significance contributed negatively to the public's attitudes, irrespective of whether they were for or against nuclear energy. He concluded "the policy makers underestimated the public's negative evaluation of psychological risks and they also underestimated the public's belief that the use of nuclear energy would lead to such risks.[20]

Otway argued that to expect people's attitudes to be determined by statistical estimates of physical safety is highly simplified and is based on an incorrect model of the human thought process, implying an unreal degree of "rationality." His studies suggested people are responding in a "rational" sense by integrating information in terms of their own subjective values and choosing to respond in a way consistent with those values.[21] His analysis of public opinion clearly showed the nuclear debate is not simply concerned with facts, or costs and benefits in the usual sense, but with psychological and social factors as well. The latter reflect concerns with centralization of scarce resources, such as energy, the control of these resources by impersonal bureaucracies, and public resentment of a growing dependence on the specialized knowledge of a technocratic elite.[22] In a sense, nuclear energy may be serving as a psychological symbol of what is really a larger discussion about the appropriateness of further technological developments, the complexities and uncertainties of modern life, and a lack of confidence in social institutions.

A French study also made clear reference to the impact of psychological forces on people's attitudes toward nuclear energy. In addressing the risks of accidents and their consequences, the author pointed out how the concept of risk refers to both the probability of occurrence of a damaging event and the subsequent damage intensity. The author argued that while probability of occurrence can be calculated, the damage intensity as perceived by individuals remained subjective and "close to ancestral fears, hardly pervaded with risk rationalization."[23]

Another author postulated that people's anxieties about nuclear weapons are now being displaced onto nuclear power in general, which provides an object more easily accessible on a conscious level. He argued that the intensity of emotions directed toward nuclear power may be a displacement of unconscious fears of nuclear weapons.[24]

In concluding this review, it is clear that the issues around nuclear developments have entered the consciousness of people around the globe and have been responded to with common psychological concerns. The Austrian debate highlighted people's concerns with feeling unsafe and vulnerable around nuclear plants, susceptible to accidents at the hands of technology or terrorists. There is throughout the world an expression by people of fear, fears of future generations being damaged by exposure to radiation if an accident would occur and fears of bequeathing a poisonous future in the form of toxic, radioactive waste.

Furthermore, there is also a more difficult to identify type of fear that springs from what may be an association of nuclear technological developments with nuclear weapons. This fear raises concerns over the destructive potential of nuclear radiation and reflects the fears of annihilation and destruction associated with nuclear weapons.

It is clear that despite attempts by nuclear proponents to alleviate these fears, they will not vanish. These fears appear deeply rooted and express people's attempts at adjusting to unknown and overwhelming technologic changes. It behooves both the purveyors of this technology and ourselves to confront these fears so we may be able to help people cope with and adjust to the changing world and the new dangers it brings. Addressing these fears will help us all stop and examine closely the dilemmas nuclear developments pose and whether the risks are truly worthwhile.

References

1. Hirsch H: The nuclear energy information campaign of the Austrian government. Proceedings of IAEA, May 2-13, 1977, Vol 7, Nuclear Power and Public Opinion and Safeguards, CNC 36/589, pp 219-236

2. International Atomic Energy Association: Nuclear controversy in Austria 1976-1977: a review. 1979, pp 1-45
3. *Ibid,* pp 3-6
4. *Ibid,* p 10
5. *Ibid,* pp 12-20
6. *Ibid,* pp 22-29
7. Hallerbach J: The true 'cone' splitting: trade unions and citizen groups on conflict over nuclear power. Darmstadt, Germany, Sammlung Luchterhand, 1978, p 241
8. Bellelli U: Italian attidues and public opinion toward nuclear power stations, in Uranium Supply and Demand: Proceedings of Third International Symposium. London, Mining Journal Books, 1978, pp 249-252
9. Elstub J, et al: Nuclear power: advantages that outweigh the risks. Atom, April 1978, pp 103-106
10. Nemoto K: Content analysis on controversy on nuclear safety issues. Nippon Gershiryoku Gakki-Shi, February 1978, pp 96-102
11. Nemoto K: Site and social assessments of nuclear power plants. Dengyoku Doboku, September 1977, pp 44-50
12. Inai R: Reprocessing of Spent Fuel and Public Acceptance. Tokyo, I.S.U., 1977, pp 205-215
13. Yamada T, Ohori H: Public acceptance of nuclear power development in Japan, in Proceedings of International Conference on Nuclear Power, May 2-13, 1977, Vol 7 Salzburg, Austria, IAEA, pp 185-195
14. *Ibid,* pp 192-193
15. *Ibid,* p 195
16. Otway HJ: The perception of technological risks: a psychological perspective, in Technological Risk: Its Perceptions and Handling in the European Community Proceedings, CEC/CERD, Berlin, April 1-3, 1979, pp 1-10
17. Otway HJ: Review of research on identification of factors influencing social response to technological risks, in Proceedings of International Conference on Nuclear Power, May 2-13, 1977 Salzburg, Austria, CN 36/4 pp 95-118
18. Otway HJ: The perception of technological risks, *op cit,* pp 1-10
19. Otway HJ, Maurer D, Thomas K: Nuclear power: the question of public acceptance. Futures, April 1978, pp 109-118
20. Thomas K, Gwaton E, Fishburn M, Otway HJ: Nuclear energy: the accuracy of policy makers' perceptions of public beliefs, Research Report 80-18. Laxenburg, Austria, International Institute for Applied Systems Analysis, 1980, pp 1-24
21. Otway HJ, Maurer D, Thomas K: *op cit,* pp 116-117
22. *Ibid,* p 117
23. Gouvenet A: Risks of accidents and their consequences. Radioprotection 12z:131-142, 1977
24. Pahner P: A psychological perspective on the nuclear energy controversy, RM76-67. Laxenburg, Austria, International Institute for Applied Systems Analysis, 1975

THE IMPACT ON CHILDREN AND ADOLESCENTS OF NUCLEAR DEVELOPMENTS

William Beardslee, M.D. and
John Mack, M.D.

Both nuclear power and nuclear weapons have become realities in the lifetimes of many of us. We know somehow that our futures, whether we like it or not, are bound up with the development of nuclear weapons and the use or non-use of such weapons. Children are even more vulnerable because their lives will be longer, they are more at risk from radiation, and they have little control or power over what may happen to them.

Very little literature exists on the psychosocial impacts of nuclear developments on children, not least of all because most adults probably don't recognize that a child could indeed be concerned about nuclear developments or have opinions worth soliciting on the subject. In responding to this lack, this Task Force has attempted to sample children's attitudes toward nuclear weapons and nuclear power, trying to see whether these are concerns for children, and, if so, what the nature of the concerns might be. Following is a survey of papers; a brief examination of a few relevant works from the adult literature; a report of our questionnaire findings; and a discussion of the results: concerns about the psychosocial impacts of living in the nuclear age.

Part I: Literature Review

Compared with the substantial amount of research done around the immediate and long-term physical and physiological effects of nuclear technology, little continuous research has been undertaken on psychosocial impacts, and even less on psychosocial effects on children. Our review of the literature showed lack of materials in two specific areas. First, research concerning *what children think* has been neglected. While a few studies have looked at children and war through the use of questionnaires, there are no interview studies, no studies conducted with the parents, very few attitudinal surveys (and most of those were conducted before 1967), and almost no theoretical papers. The other area of inadequate research concerns the developmental *effects* of the threat of war on children psychologically and socially.

We have divided our review into two parts, a review of particularly relevant work on adults and a review of the literature on children.

A. The Relevant Literature on Adults

1. The Atom Bomb Literature

Probably the most significant contribution to our understanding of the effects of nuclear war has been the post–World War II studies and testimonies of the atom bomb victims in Japan. Nearly thirty-five years after the bombs were dropped, physiological investigations of the actual and residual effects of radiation on the survivors are still underway.

However, most of the atom bomb literature focused on testimonials (e.g., Summer Cloud)[1] and on the medical and physiological aspects (e.g., eye disease, cancer/ leukemia, blood disorders, skin problems, genetic mutations) with significantly little mention of the psychosocial effects.

As far as the social and psychological effects are concerned, the effort made so far to investigate them is pitiful.[2]

This report by the Natural Science Group, published in the *Bulletin of the Atomic Scientists* in December 1977, also stated:

. . . communities disintegrated. The social services collapsed. Many people went mad or committed suicide. . . . Fear of malformed offspring often prevents marriages, and unusual susceptibility to disease and fatigue often threatens employment . . .[3]

Yet the works which address these psychosocial issues continue to be few.

Robert J. Lifton's important and compassionate chronicle *Death in Life* presented an initial step toward investigation of the psychosocial effects of the atom bomb on the Japanese people.

> One effect the atomic bombings had upon the Japanese, I soon discovered, was to create an intensity of feeling which could interfere with evaluating their human impact. . . . I discovered that despite the 17 years that had passed since the bomb, no Japanese individual or group had carried out a detailed or systematic study of its general psychological and social effects.[4]

Lifton's research on Hiroshima and Nagasaki suggested the phenomenon "psychic closing off," (or "psychic shutdown, psychic numbing,")

> The survivor's major defense against death anxiety and death guilt is the cessation of feeling . . . psychic closing off also suppresses the survivor's rage.[5]

Lifton described the overall psychological effects on survivors or *hibakushas* (the Japanese word for "explosion-affected person or persons"):

> We thus encounter in both Hiroshima and concentration camp survivors, what can be called a pervasive tendency toward sluggish despair—a more or less permanent form of psychic numbing which includes diminished vitality, chronic depression and constricted life space, and which covers over the rage and mistrust that are just beneath the surface.[6]

> . . . the antisocial behavior which may occur in an atomic bomb orphan is merely one extreme expression of the general experience of all who are exposed to the bomb: of a vast breakdown of faith in the larger human matrix supporting each individual life, and therefore a loss of faith (or trust) in the structure of human existence.[7]

It is clear that there is a devastating, profound, life-long psychological impact of being the target of an atomic bomb, that one's sense of self and security is profoundly shaken, however powerful and eloquent some of the survivors may be in describing the ways they have lived through it. People are still struggling to come to grips with what happened at Hiroshima and are deeply disturbed by it, even 35 years later. The lack of psychological research beyond Lifton's work, we feel, is related in part, as Lifton himself suggested, to the incomprehensibility of the horror and a denying of what happened and what it may have cost.

2. Overall Perspective on Adults

A major work addressing the overall psychological aspects of the threat of nuclear war is the Group for the Advancement of Psychiatry (GAP) report, Psychiatric Aspects of the Prevention of Nuclear War, published in 1964. It presents work done on attitudes toward war and the presence of nuclear armaments in light of world conflict. We feel it is a concise summary of psychological principles that are relevant to education of children and informed public debate on nuclear weapons.

The report's recurrent theme is that nuclear technology has transformed the nature of war—the fact that existing nuclear arsenals are capable of eliminating life as we know it changes the "givens" of war—and yet our thought patterns have not responded to these new conditions. This gap is maintained by psychological factors such as *denial* or the inability to comprehend what has not been experienced.

The operative psychological factors are many and complex. Old ways of coping no longer work.

> Recourse to war traditionally has been a way of protecting national security, interests and ideals; now, however, nuclear war incurs the risk of national suicide. . . .[8]

> War, which once met the basic human psychological needs of aggressiveness and social cohesiveness, has become irrelevant to these needs.[9]

Instead, perhaps war in and of itself is so fearsome that psychically we have "turned it off," as was discussed earlier in connection with Lifton's work. In order to cope with the complexity and the potential immense devastation of nuclear war, we tend to dehumanize the enemy.

The distance between the "enemy" and individuals increases and war is dehumanized with push button technology. Couple this with the *need* for dehumanization as a coping mechanism in the face of the magnitude of the new reality which surrounds us. To prevent psychological and cognitive "overkill" we blur the potential for destructive and constructive human consequences of the new technologies . . .[10]

The implications and effects of this need to be explored in that continued use of dehumanization as a protective pattern will prevent the "kind of social action and/or administrative responsibility that could have a meaningful effect on (a person's) individual and social destinies."[11]

The concern of the GAP report thus becomes the prevention of war with an emphasis on education of values and communication skills which will teach children and adults how to carry on meaningful forms of conflict and disagreement without resorting to violence.

Dr. Jerome Frank, a member of our Task Force, expanded some of these points in *Sanity and Survival*. Frank pointed out that in the past the more weapons a nation possessed, the more secure and powerful it was. Today with nuclear weapons the concept of "protection through military superiority" has become meaningless. Frank moved on to focus on the motivations for war and the various psychological effects of preparation for nuclear war. Thus his conclusion was in accordance with the GAP report:

Survival today depends on reducing, controlling, channeling and redirecting the drive for power and the impulse to violence and fostering the countervailing drives toward fellowship and community.[12]

What the GAP report and Dr. Frank's work emphasize is that, in view of the arms race, new ways of thinking are necessary and that defensive processes such as denial, dehumanization, and perceiving nuclear war in the context of traditional war make reasonable public debate and decision-making nearly impossible.

B. Review of the Literature on Children

1. Nuclear War and Children

The specific area of the psychological effects of war and thinking of war on children has been addressed by only a few, using questionnaires and surveys. The formative considerations of Sibylle Escalona in "Children and the Threat of Nuclear War" offered valuable speculation, although the data have limitations.

The focus of Escalona's work was the impact of nuclear danger upon the development of aspects of personality in children. Escalona and a group of colleagues conducted a questionnaire survey of children from ages four to adolescence in which they were asked what they thought the world would be like by the time they grew up. Now the total sample, more than 70 percent, spontaneously mentioned nuclear weapons and destructive war as a likely possibility. A relatively high proportion expressed pessimism about the future. This led Escalona to conclude that there was a severe influence on developmental processes in normal children because of the threats posed by nuclear weapons and nuclear war. However, as she stated in her article, this conclusion was speculative and the data itself was flawed by the fact that the samplings of children were quite varied and the questions asked of children also varied depending on which particular examiner posed them. However, Escalona was convinced that a

> profound uncertainty about whether or not mankind has a foreseeable future exerts a corrosive and malignant influence upon important development processes in normal and well-functioning children.[13]

Understanding identification and the establishment of personal identity to be the developmental focus of the school-age child, Escalona proposed that the threat of nuclear war "weakens and impedes" these processes.

> Young people come to terms with the adult world as long as it holds out a reasonable promise for fulfillment in some spheres of living.[14]

If the future seems in doubt to the child, and if adult models appear to feel inadequate to cope with the dangers of nuclear war, and hence appear unable to ensure a future, Escalona asked where is the pull for maturity?

Another study was conducted in 1965 by Milton Schwebel entitled "Nuclear Cold War: Student Opinions and Professional Responsibility."[15] Questionnaires were given to 3,000 students, mostly from junior and high schools, of various socioeconomic backgrounds. The questionnaires dealt with children's views on war and civil defense.

The results of Schwebel's survey showed that children do know and *care* about the threat of thermonuclear war and that they know and *fear* the dangers of nuclear disaster. However, this survey, according to Schwebel, offered no valid measure of the degree to which such "mental anguish has been converted to pathology." Schwebel felt war not only influenced children's morality and interpersonal relations, but also created insecurity and therefore influenced children's perceptions of social order and future expectations.

The results of insecurities caused two possible responses in youth, according to Schwebel: 1) to face the facts of war and live with the "erosive effects" of fear; or 2) to avoid the facts and *deny* thought and understanding processes. To counter either of these effects and maintain health, Schwebel suggested several steps, one focus being an active involvement toward effecting peace.

"Children and War," a position paper written by Law in 1971 for the Association for Childhood Education International, surveyed children's and adult's attitudes as presented in current literature with a particular interest to what children were being taught. She concluded:

> Children are apparently still being taught to think of organized killing of human beings by other human beings as a natural and perhaps noble part of human experience.[16]

In light of the GAP report findings on the dehumanization of war, coupled with the ambivalences felt in adults about war, Law's finding is deeply disturbing.

The final grouping of research, conducted through surveys (and mentioned in Law's paper also), are those which focus on the development of political attitudes in children. Most of these studies have been done by Judith

Torney and associates. Their hypotheses and findings closely link with the speculations being discussed by Escalona and Schwebel.

One study by Hess and Torney concluded that a child's involvement with the political system starts with a strong positive attachment to the country. The U.S. is seen as

> ideal and as superior to other countries; the child perceives figures and institutions of government as powerful, competent, benign and infallible and trusts them to offer him protection and help.[17]

These ties and confidence in the country are seen as important in socialization and as deriving from complex psychological and social needs.

Hess and Torney also mentioned that, in viewing politics, especially the relationship between two parties and the conduct of elections, children wish to minimize conflict. By the eighth grade, children see the need for consensus and for majority rule.

> Despite the decline in the personal respect for authority figures, a basic regard for the roles of authority in the system and for the competence necessary to perform these roles seems not to diminish.[18]

(This statement was made in 1967, and may not be so true today.)

The findings of a more recent work (1976) by Buergenthal and Torney also presented pertinent information. They concluded that:

1. Children tend to see peace as an *absence of war* rather than an active process of conflict resolution and cooperation;
2. Many see war as inevitable, necessary, and likely.[19]

2. Nuclear Technology and Children

In addition to the international literature cited above, Slovic and Luskin conducted studies on public attitudes toward nuclear technology. Slovic did not focus particularly on children, though he did sample a group of students from the University of Oregon in Eugene. In brief, his results showed that nuclear power was rated most "risky" and comparable to the risk of motor vehicle accidents. Second to these in risk was handguns. The *benefits* of nuclear power appeared unappreciated.

Slovic emphasized the "gap" between the opinions of technical experts and lay people and suggested that there were two reasons for the perpetuation of this gap. One is technological—even the experts are still debating the "facts" about nuclear energy. The other reason is psychological, with the primary dynamic termed "availability heuristic," a dynamic which blurs the distinction between what is "remotely possible and what is probable," by exaggerating the facts via imagination.[20]

Slovic said that the public's response to X rays shows that a radiation technology *can* be tolerated once it is familiar, its benefits clear, and its practitioners trusted. However, the unresolved technical issues in the risk assessment process of nuclear power, coupled with the mental processes of "availability heuristic," constitute a block at present to changes in attitude toward nuclear power. We saw that a crisis such as the oil shortage in 1973–1974 could cause the public to accept higher risk technologies. People are generally willing to accept increased risks in exchange for increased benefits. However, as Slovic stated, the psychological effects of such crisis-induced acceptance of nuclear energy could have high cost for the American people:

> Such crisis-induced acceptance of nuclear power may, however, produce anxiety and stress in a population forced to tolerate what it perceives as a great risk because of its addiction to the benefits of electricity.[21]

It is unlikely that young children, say below the age of eight, are caught up in risk-benefit analyses of nuclear technology. In addition, their understanding of risk-benefit relationships is probably mediated to a large extent by their parents. However, Slovic's dynamic "availability heuristic" has sharp implications for children, especially in relationship to their mechanism of imagination. The "fact" of a small leak at a nuclear plant might plant a seed of anxiety in the mind of a child that imagination could then nourish.

Luskin and his associates also addressed the issue of public attitudes toward physical and biological risks of radiation and the benefits of nuclear power plants.[22] Two towns were used—one near a nuclear plant under construction, one not so near a plant—and young people were included in the sample. Four levels were surveyed: elementary (6th grade); junior high school (8th grade); high school (11th grade); and faculty (public schools). Because of reading level differences, two surveys were used, one for the elementary children and one for all others.

Among the students, no significant patterns emerged that could be attributed to developmental or age categories. The largest response to whether the government sets "safe limits" was "sometimes." (This response came from all groups.) The overall results of the survey indicate a general lack of understanding of sources and types of radiation, a lack of understanding of biological effects, and a lack of confidence in the "experts."[23]

Part II: A.P.A. Task Force Questionnaire Results

Our review of the literature convinced us that basically little is known about what young people feel about nuclear weapons and nuclear power, and we embarked on our study assuming that our youth were relatively isolated from the nuclear debate. However, as we gathered data, it became clear that young people are deeply concerned about the issues, and that many are able to provide strong and often eloquent answers to our questions. Youth do not mainly resort to denial and "psychic shutdown."

As a group, we designed a questionnaire which was subsequently administered to grammar and high school students.

Figure 1 presents the questions that were used in the first administration of the questionnaire. Subsequent refinements in wording have been made, but the basic content areas have remained the same. The aim of the questionnaire was to sample a range of relevant attitudes toward nuclear weapons and nuclear power. Students were encouraged to respond in depth to the questions.

The questionnaire was administered to school students by members of the Task Force in the areas in which they lived—Los Angeles, Boston, Baltimore and Philadelphia, and responses were pooled and analyzed together. Qualitative analysis was performed only on questionnaires circulated by Drs. Mack and Beardslee in the Boston area. Clearly, this represents a first step, not a final answer to the question of what are children's attitudes toward nuclear power and nuclear weapons. It is not a systematic population survey in any standard epidemiological sense. Nonetheless, because of the diversity of ages, educational background, and areas of the country within the sample, as well as the size of the sample, we feel the findings *are* a beginning and raise important questions.

We also feel that both a qualitative and quantitative analysis of the results are necessary. A qualitative presentation is needed not only because of the relative lack of information in this area but also because, while going over the questionnaires, we were impressed repeatedly by the eloquence and power of a number of the students' answers. We feel that, in general, both the quantitative and the qualitative analyses suggest strongly that children are aware of and deeply concerned about nuclear weapons and nuclear power.

Figure 1

1. What does the word "nuclear" bring to mind?
2. Have you participated in any activity related to nuclear technology?
3. How old were you when you were first aware of nuclear advances? Discuss what you thought then and now.
4. What are the benefits and dangers of nuclear power plants in your area? How do you feel about nuclear power?
5. How important do you feel nuclear weapons are for our national security?
6. What do you think about civil defense? (Bombshelters, sandbagging industries, evacuation plans?)
7. Do you think that you could survive a nuclear attack? Your city? Your country?
8. If a neighboring city was being held and blackmailed

by a terrorist group with a powerful thermonuclear weapon, how would you feel?

9. Have thermonuclear advances influenced your plans for marriage, having children, or planning for the future?

10. Have thermonuclear advances affected your way of thinking? (About the future, your view of the world, time?)

A: Qualitative Analysis

Questionnaires were presented to about 75 students with specific encouragement to respond in detail. There was close supervision of the administration process. (Dr. Mack was present in the classroom while the questionnaires were filled out, and Dr. Beardslee gave a lecture after the forms were completed.) Responses presented here show the range of comments of students. The criterion for selection was the clarity or eloquence of the statement, not political content or position. The students whose statements are reported here studied at a private high school in the Boston area or a public high school north of Boston, and all students were in the 10th, 11th or 12th grades. The questionnaires were collected in 1978 for the qualitative response, although for the larger sample used in the quantitative analysis the collection period extended from 1978 to 1980. We feel that the individual responses reported are representative of the sample from which they are drawn.

1. What does the word "nuclear" bring to mind?

Big gray clouds, pipes and smokestacks, red warning lights, dead wildlife and humans, unnecessary deaths and bodies.

A huge white cloud of smoke covering the area, Russia bombing us, danger, radioactivity, wars, death.

Fission, fusion, power (constructive and destructive), meltdown, Hiroshima, Nagasaki, leak, explosion, radiation, cancer.

Bombs, the world as nothing, completely wiped out.

Danger, death, sadness, corruption, explosion, cancer, children, waste, bombs, pollution, terrible, terrible devaluing of human life.

Energy, warmth, modern plant, power source, danger, risk, heat.

Energy, society, advances, bombs exploding, people dying, buildings ruined, society demolished, big wars between countries.

Nuclear means a source of energy which could provide the world with energy needed for future generations. It also means the destruction of marine life whose environment is ruined by nuclear waste. Also the destruction of human lives when used in missiles.

Energy, helping to cut down on the overseas expense of fuel (which will eventually help our economy), oil and gas are going to run out eventually. We need something else to lean back on for our own survival.

Stars, planets, space, darkness.

All that comes to mind is the world's final demise. A total kind of holocaust. The world will be killed by all nuclear devices. Also, I think of very dangerous unlimited energy.

2. Have you participated in any activity related to nuclear technology?

I read a booklet called Hiroshima in which individuals who survived this destruction discussed the horrible effects the bomb had then and how it affected their futures.

A close relation is an electrical engineer and was largely involved with some nuclear trials (not quite sure to determine what); hired by the U.S. Government, but definitely have had pro-nuclear input to my ideas.

No, but I have read the articles in the paper telling about the pros and cons of the plant. The papers have told about both sides of this idea of creating energy.

In my 9th grade geography class we studied alterntive sources of energy and listed the pros and cons of having nuclear power plants.

3. How old were you when you were first aware of nuclear advances? Discuss what you thought then and now.

I was pretty small when my parents first told me stories of bombs that could blow up countries. It just seems too unreal.

When I was younger, nuclear energy did not impress me. It still does not impress me. I feel that if the world at large is going to play with nuclear devices they should first be concerned with the safety factors.

I thought of a great power only used in bombs or submarines—only used for military. Now I think of it as a dangerous but necessary form of power that the U.S. will have to use until solar, wind, geothermal, and other non-fossil forms of power are efficient enough to supply the nation.

I first became aware of nuclear advances when controversy grew around the Seabrook plant—ten miles away from my home. Despite the fact that it is located in New Hampshire, I feel that nearby Massachusetts residents should have a say in its construction because it will affect us, too.

I was 13 and felt that they were terrible, dangerous, and that no good could come from them but rather only massive destruction. I am now 15 and I feel that nuclear power is a great breakthrough and will be very useful as a source of the nation's energy in future years.

When I was about eight, I watched a news broadcast on the anniversary of Hiroshima, showing the bombing and devastation. Always through grade school we would be shown where the bomb shelter was, just in case. Then I was less informed and thus thought less on the subject but as I learned more and more, I became more and more negative toward the whole thing.

I was probably ten or eleven, and all I thought of was "blowing up places" with bombs. I didn't realize that nuclear power could be used for things other than bombs. Now, I think nuclear power could be a very important asset, but first we should find a safe way to use it and dispose of the waste.

I first became aware in the third grade. It was all part of men going to the moon, clean energy, no more smog—now I think that it's clean when it works and when it doesn't it's far worse. It would probably be okay if they put up strict (very strict) regulations about safety, but even if they wrote the regulations no one would go by them.

It was only a few years ago when I became aware of nuclear power. I believe it was Hiroshima that I'd heard of although I didn't know the name of the town at the time. I remember feeling sad and bitter at belonging to a race that would do such things. Since then my knowledge has grown and I continue to become more and more disgusted—although not hopeless, yet.

I believe I was in junior high when I first became aware. Of course, I found it terrifying as every human being in that our whole world, my whole world, could be destroyed by one bomb that our nation had first discovered. A bomb that every advanced civilization sought to obtain. To destroy our own race, to destroy people, culture, life and earth is essentially the outcome of the A-Bomb.

4. What are the benefits and dangers of nuclear power plants in your area? How do you feel about it?

Benefits of plants—new source of energy, new jobs. Dangers—possible explosions, nuclear waste, pollution of waters. The dangers are more important.

We would definitely see a decrease in the heating bills but it is a touchy process. If there is just a slight chance that it could explode, sends me into paranoia.

In Seabrook there is a new nuclear power plant that poses a big threat to our area if something goes wrong; however, it has brought new jobs and promises to make more efficient and less expensive energy for our community.

The benefits may be of less taxes since the plant is in your town. The explosions may be a disadvantage. I don't believe in nuclear energy.

The dangers would occur if any nuclear power slipped out into the ocean or the air it would harm people and animal life. The benefit would only be that nuclear power would be here so we could use it. I feel that it would be better to get rid of the nuclear plants in order to save the living things around us. We should do away with the increased risk of death by doing away with the nuclear plants.

The benefits are that there would be more energy available to use and it might be cheaper since we live so close. The dangers are that living so close to the Seabrook plant, if anything happens, such as a nuclear explosion, I don't think we would have any chance of surviving. Also, it would make the ocean around here five degrees warmer which will hurt us ecologically.

The benefits of nuclear power plants are jobs, supply of energy. The dangers are possible radioactive harm to people in surrounding areas, harm to environment in the ocean where the water temperature is changed and hurts the environment, which may harm our ocean food supply and hurt fishermen and also the danger of what to do with nuclear wastes that remain radioactive. The risk should not be taken.

The benefit is that we won't have to rely on the Arab nations for all of our energy. We will be able to supply almost all of our own energy. The danger that is turning a lot of people away from the plant is the chance of an explosion. This explosion would ruin everything in this area.

There aren't many benefits to the nuclear plant except that we may get a little more energy to help run this country with, but besides that, all the results are bad. We could all be blown away very quickly if someone did one little thing to disturb it. All the plants and animals are going to die because of all the stuff going into the air and we could be subject to getting cancer. The fish will all die and our beaches will be contaminated.

The benefits are the energy that it supplied to us and the use of nuclear power in warfare. The dangers are the massive destructive of aquatic creatures and the possibility of a radiation leakage and also the possibility of sabotage.

I think the ignorant are easily delusioned to the safety of these plants.

There are no benefits—only rate hikes. The dangers are numerous. The plants are not needed—we have already an excess of energy. I don't understand why we continue in this progression toward death.

5. How important do you feel nuclear weapons are for our national security?

If others have them we need them or we will not stay on top. The U.S. does *not* want to be pushed around. I like our freedom.

I don't see any sense to them if we have to have them; what good is having enough to blow up the world nine times—it's senseless. We wouldn't solve anything, just kill ourselves.

The whole idea of nuclear weapons makes me shudder. They will only serve to wipe man off this planet. The bombs and nuclear warheads are only garbage. National security wouldn't be important if people had more understanding.

For the present definition of national security, very; in reality none whatsoever.

I think they are important in that they keep a balance of power so that no one country can feel safe to attack other places.

I feel we should be able to settle things in an intelligent way. I don't agree with weapons and killing.

Nuclear weapons are only important for our national morale and ego. If we continue to keep nuclear weapons, we will grow to live in a false sense of security. We will become oblivious to the fact that other countries have nuclear weapons too and use of them in war time can only lead to a nuclear holocaust of perhaps the entire earth.

I think the U.S. should have on hand enough weapons to protect itself and the rest of the free world. This makes nuclear arms very important. If we allow our armies to become inferior then our nation is in peril. We should remain militarily superior to all nations who oppose our ideas which means if nuclear arms are used in other nations we must have better nuclear arms. We have the intelligence to use them only when absolutely necessary.

I feel it's good to have a strong security and defense for our country, but I'm not sure if nuclear weapons are the answer. It won't be too long now before most major countries have nuclear weapons and if there's another big war, you can say goodbye to most major cities or countries or even the world.

I think nuclear weapons are very necessary for our national security if we intend to remain a major power. We have to keep up.

I think that nuclear weapons are completely unnecessary for protection of the U.S. All they do is cause more death and destruction. If there was a nuclear war right now, the earth probably wouldn't survive it.

Nuclear weapons are kind of stupid. If a lot of countries or one country has one it doesn't matter because if one is used we're going to die anyway. I feel if we have another world war it will probably be the destruction of our race and earth itself.

If we did not have nuclear weapons, this country would be part of Russia or China.

I hope we don't ever come to using weapons. I think there are better ways of killing people than burning them slowly.

I don't think the U.S. public or the Russian public would stand for their government to "push the button." I hope the human race is not stupid enough to destroy themselves. Nuclear weapons put too much power into few hands.

As long as we, as human beings, tend toward brutal conflict, and as long as the Russians have the weapons, I see our national security extremely dependent upon nuclear weapons.

I realize that without the power of nuclear weapons our nation would not hold the strength it does today. Yet what good does it do us to have a bomb to kill a nation that has already destroyed us.

6. What do you think about civil defense? (Bombshelters, sandbagging industries, evacuation plans?)

I think in this day and age it is utterly ridiculous not to have them. What if there should be an emergency. We also should know how to get to them quickly and easily and we must be taught.

I guess they're a good idea for those whom would rather just survive for their own reasons. If only a few people could be saved I wouldn't want to be one of them to be alone to start a new world over.

If we were ever to have a nuclear war, the entire world's population could be destroyed thus making civil defense useless to us right now and in the future.

Are alright if everyone has them but it isn't fair because some can afford them.

I feel that civil defense is important if the power plant blows up or is destroyed. But I don't know if bomb shelters, evacuation plans, etc. will be sturdy enough to save us all.

7. Do you think that you could survive a nuclear attack? Your city? Your country?

Very doubtful.

I really don't think we could and even if some of us did, the side effects from it would be awful. Remember, there are still people today suffering from the effects of Hiroshima.

We could try but I think that ultimately we would be destroyed.

Well, yes, if the attack occurred 100 or so miles away. It would definitely devastate the area it hit, so a city being hit would not survive. The country would not be completely wiped out, only a large part. Well, actually, the country could be wiped out.

No! With all the bombs that could be let off there would be nothing to come back to even if we could stay in a bomb shelter.

No—personally; my city—no; my country—possibly.

I have no idea, it's hard to picture New York City

being attacked by nuclear means. This generation (18, 19 years old) has not experienced any disasters or depressions. We've been comfortable, so to imagine this is very hard.

No. No. No. Some people might live, but that couldn't really be called surviving the attack.

No, even if we weren't killed we'd all have cancer in 30 years and our kids would be mutants (not to forget what the land would be like!)

At this point in time it is most probable that our city could not survive a nuclear attack. I don't think I know a single family who stores food in a fallout shelter—just in case. Perhaps a portion of the country might survive a nuclear attack—but that, too, is extremely doubtful. We often underestimate the power that the U.S.S.R. has.

I think about that often. I really don't think they could survive one whereas I am so close to one. My city would be demolished and the country in big trouble. We really don't know. It hasn't happened yet. Let's hope and pray it doesn't.

8. If a neighboring city was being held and blackmailed by a terrorist group with a powerful thermonuclear weapon, how would you feel?

Extremely frightened. I would hope that every one could evacuate the city to some other distant country.

Very scared! They would have the whole world in their hands and with a weak mind it could be a holocaust.

Not good.

I might move to Canada. I'd feel like it would be just the beginning.

Very frightened although that just doesn't seem possible to me. I would fight with everything I had, but you can't fight a nuclear bomb.

Like this whole thing had gone too far and it was imperative to surrender our nuclear weapons. Principle is not terribly important when death actually faces us. We shouldn't start a war to show our power.

I would wonder what the world was coming to.

Scared out of my mind, helpless, questionable about the human race.

9. Have thermonuclear advances influenced your plans for marriage, having children, or planning for the future?

Not in the least.

I don't choose to bring up children in a world of such horrors and dangers of deformation.

The world might be gone in two seconds from now, but I still plan for the future, because I'm going to live as long as I'm going to live.

Yes. I question my previous assumption that I will have children due to the possibility of bringing them into a world of nuclear war.

They have made me live a little more day to day knowing any time I might not be around.

No, because I haven't really thought about children or marriage. I just want to go to college. I think kids today are wild and I'd be afraid to undertake the responsibility of a child. I'm not shirking responsibility, but we're messed up now (maybe it's me) so imagine what kids would be like.

No. I don't think that worrying about these things is going to help any. I'm just going to keep on going and hope for the best.

These advances could change the way I think about having kids. They would or might have to live in a more thermonuclear city. It probably wouldn't be a good life for them.

Yes, in the way that the future doesn't seem so secure, right now I don't plan to have children—mostly for other reasons.

10. Have thermonuclear advances affected your way of thinking? (About the future, your view of the world, time?)

I am constantly aware that at any second the world might blow up in my face. It makes living more interesting.

I don't really worry about it, but it's terrifying to think that the world may not be here in a half-hour. But I'm still going to live for now.

I am strongly against it because the people who are in control of it are not worth trusting the whole world in their hands! It's much too much power for one person to hold.

I think that, unless we do something about nuclear weapons, the world and the human race may not have much time left. (corny, huh?)

It gives me a pretty dim view of the world and mankind, but it hasn't really influenced me.

How should I know? I've grown up living with it. The bomb was dropped on Hiroshima and Nagasaki 16 years before I was born.

I have now accepted the fact that there quite possibly will be an "end of time."

Everything has to be looked at on two levels: the world with the threat of ending soon, and life with future, etc. The former has to be blocked out for everyday functioning because very few people can find justification in living otherwise. But the latter is always there—on a much larger scale than possibilities of individual deaths—car accidents, etc., even though the result to me, personally, would be the same.

It just makes me realize how fast our world is advancing. I know it will affect me a great deal when I get older because I plan on going into politics or social sciences and there will be much disagreement then. I want to advance to help ourselves but I'm scared of the unknown.

Yes, probably a little. It makes you wonder about how anyone could even dare to hurt others so badly.

I feel our growth is speeding up and if we don't slow down then we're going to die. These advances are too quick and they seem to be taking over our world.

For me, life goes on. I, myself, try to be aware of the world around me, get involved, etc., but sometimes I'd rather sit back and live and let live. I'm very confused by current issues—I just can't make up my mind to side with pro or con.

The concept of nuclear energy impresses me and I

think in the future it will be practical for much use if it is desired. Where once I thought the world everlasting and would be around long after humans would, I now have doubts. Time is not affected by nuclear energy but my life span may be affected.

I think that a nuclear war, which could break out in a relatively short period of time in the far future, could nearly destroy the world.

In a way it has. It has shown me how stupid some adults can be. If they know it could easily kill them I have no idea why they support it. Once in a while it makes me start to think that the end of my time in life may not be as far off as I would like it to be.

Yes, we are a nation in progress, a world in progress; we need to hope for the better, and think better.

Yes, I feel if men keep going on with experiments they are bound to make one mistake that could mean the end of a lot of surrounding cities and if severe enough the end of what we know today as the world.

B: Quantitative analysis

For quantitative analysis, all questionnaires collected between 1978 and 1980 were used. Altogether 1,151 questionnaires were examined. The questionnaire underwent some revisions in 1979 and 1980, in order to facilitate quantitative scoring. Thus three separate samples were examined first: those from 1978 (434 children) grades 5 to 12, (mostly concentrated in the younger grades), 1979 (389 high school students), and 1980 (328 high school students). Most of these were from urban and suburban areas in Los Angeles, Boston, and Baltimore. Both public and private schools were represented, although the majority were from public schools. Scoring consisted of assigning responses to one of several predetermined categories and then calculating the precentage of the group in a sample responding in that particular category. Given the preliminary nature of the study and the difficulties of assigning open-ended responses to discrete categories, there were a fair number of unscorable answers. The major trends across samples are reported here, with a few examples from specific samples as indicated. We have not attempted to analyze the questionnaires for trends between the years 1978 and 1980. We did analyze one sample, Sample Three, carefully for age and sex trends within the sample. The few significant results encountered are presented in the following discussion.

Findings

Few children thought about the technical or scientific uses of nuclear technology when asked about what the word "nuclear" brings to mind. Most thought either of nuclear weapons or nuclear energy or a combination. Quite a large number of students became aware of nuclear developments before age 12, 48 percent in the first sample, and 32 percent in the second sample, and a majority in Sample Three, demonstrating that even younger children are aware of these developments. The majority of all respondents reported that the media was the main way they became aware, followed closely by classroom information. Few had participated directly in any activity related to nuclear weapons or nuclear power. In terms of the benefits and danger of nuclear power plants, the majority of the young people questioned did not feel that there were unequivocal benefits or that safety margins were sufficient. Rather most said benefits and dangers, or simply dangers. In terms of the importance of nuclear weapons for national security, the responses were fairly evenly divided between those who felt that nuclear weapons were necessary for national security and those who felt that they were unnecessary, or who, while recognizing the need for such weapons, felt conflicted about their presence. There was considerable disagreement about the value of civil defense. Eighteen percent of Sample One considered it essential, while 35 percent felt it would not work, 31 percent were ambivalent about it, and 16 percent uncertain. In Sample Two, 53 percent considered it essential, while 14 percent questioned its value, and 14 percent were against it. The majority of all groups in Sample Three thought it worthwhile. Only in Sample One was the question asked, "Do you think that you, your city and your country could survive a nuclear attack?" And 70 percent responded that the U.S. would be ruined.

In another sample, Sample Three, the question asked, "Will there be a nuclear war?" and the majority thought

that it was at least possible, with substantially more indi-
cating it is likely. Those who felt it would occur, felt that
it was most likely to occur in the far distant future.
Another question that was asked only of Sample Three
was "Could a nuclear war be kept limited?" Over 50 percent of the girls and over 40 percent of the boys in all the
age brackets of Sample Three said it was unlikely that a
nuclear war could be kept limited. The responses to the
questions about the likelihood of nuclear terrorism occurr-
ing were varied across the samples with a significant
group, but not the majority, feeling that it was likely to
occur.

The final set of questions had to do with the overall
effects of these developments on living for the children
and adolescents involved. In Sample One radiation resulting from nuclear developments was expressed as a concern by 61 percent of those who responded, while no clear
pattern emerged in the responses about the overall effects.
In Sample Two, 50 percent felt nuclear developments had
had an effect on their thoughts about marriage and their
plans for the future, while the others did not. Twenty-one
percent felt that they had changed their feelings overall
and 29 percent were undecided. Forty percent were unclear about the manner in which the nuclear developments had affected their lives, 32 percent thought it didn't
touch them at all, 5 percent thought it had had a positive
effect, and 15 percent thought it had had a negative effect.
In Sample Three, the majority of all students sampled in all
age groups felt that thermonuclear developments had affected their thoughts about marriage and children. And
again a majority felt that thermonuclear developments had
affected their daily thinking and feeling. Over 70 percent
of the girls and about 50 percent of the boys felt that
radiation from nuclear wastes and nuclear power plants
would shorten their lives.

Part III. Discussion

Results of our questionnaire survey strongly suggest
that children are deeply disturbed about the threats of
nuclear war and the risks of nuclear power, while they also
recognize possible benefits from nuclear power and

nuclear weapons. There are many different ideas and opinions, but it is clear that certainly by the time students reach adolescence nuclear issues are of real concern. Our strongest finding, we feel, is a general unquiet or uneasiness about the future and about the present nature of nuclear weapons and nuclear power. There is a particular uncertainty and fear about nuclear war or the limiting of such a war should it occur, and the possibilities of survival.

Perhaps one might argue that children should not be drawn into discussion about nuclear weapons and nuclear power simply because they are too young to understand fully. Yet dealing with the effects of nuclear power and nuclear weapons has to be a major concern of theirs throughout their lives. Furthermore, even as children and students, they are deeply affected. They are affected by the radiation in the atmosphere from nuclear testing, perhaps more seriously than adults as their lives are potentially longer, and they will be deeply affected by decisions made in the present in which they have no say, no voice.

While we have concentrated here on what the children say themselves, clearly another major area of interest is how parents' attitudes—how the worry, concern, or sense of security that nuclear weapons and the nuclear arms race generate—are transmitted to children.

One cannot help wondering from these materials whether nuclear developments are having an impact on the very structure of personality itself in adolescence, particularly in the areas of impulse management and ego ideal organization. (It is difficult, of course, since these questionnaires specifically tapped the impact of nuclear developments, to separate out their effect on young people from that of other technological changes such as pollution, computer science, or the development of television broadcasting, which nightly brings into the home in living color the horror of disease, fire, accidents, and war.)

The ego ideal, the image we carry within of our best selves or of what we would wish to be like, is the outcome of a series of compromises a child makes with reality, starting with earliest infancy and continuing through each stage of development, between his or her wishes and desires and the appreciation that at least for the present their perfect fulfillment is not possible. The limits set by the parents upon the toddler's wish to seek and destroy, or upon the three- to five-year-old's desire to possess exclusively each of his or her parents, are among the classic disappointments of small children. There are many other similar disappointments which a child must endure, such as the realization of being small or relatively weak, or that adult sexuality and child-bearing are beyond a small girl's reach, or simply that there are other children who are smarter, better athletes, or in some respects more lovable. In adolescence, heightened sexual feeling, a desire for independence, and the development of new skills and capabilities are accompanied by the possibility of hurt and rebuff.

At each stage of development, the child mitigates disappointments by looking ahead and building a vision of the future in which he or she may possess what cannot now be had, or in which it is possible to become what he or she is incapable of being now. A healthy ego ideal builds out of possible goals or standards that are both realizable and worth struggling to achieve. But the building of such values, or of an ego ideal, depends on a present life that is perceived as stable and enduring and a future upon which the adolescent can, at least to some degree, rely.

But what happens to the ego ideal if society and its leaders are perceived cynically and the future itself is uncertain? Furthermore, how does it affect the ego ideal when the reason for that uncertainty is readily perceived to be the folly or "stupidity" of the adults around the adolescent who, because of perceived incompetence, greed, aggressiveness, lust for power, or ineffectualness can leave their children no future other than a planet contaminated by radiation and on the verge of incineration through the holocaust of nuclear war. In such a world, planning seems pointless, and ordinary values and ideals appear naive. In such a context, impulsivity, a value system of "get it now," the hyperstimulation of drugs, and the proliferation of apocalyptic cults that try to revive the idea of an afterlife while extinguishing individuality or discriminating perception, seem to be natural developments.

The emphasis in our society on immediate pleasures and satisfactions, the distrust of enduring relationships, and an unwillingness to plan for the future, as have been observed repeatedly among many of our youth in the past two decades, is often attributed to faulty child rearing practices, the abnegation of parental responsibility, or the tendency of parents to indulge their children's wishes too strongly. Perhaps there is something in this. But it needs also to be stressed that the building of enduring values within an individual depends upon the delay of present satisfactions in favor of future goals and satisfactions. But the formation of the psychic structures upon which such development depends is compromised in a setting in which the possibility of a future appears to have been destroyed by the adults to whom its preservation was ostensibly entrusted.

The preliminary findings of this study have important public policy implications. Before one can even consider these, however, it is important to stress that the experiences of these youngsters and their attitudes about nuclear energy and weapons systems cannot be welcome information to the responsible adult community. The fact that there is so little information available about how young people feel about nuclear issues that affect their lives so vitally suggests that we adults have entered into a kind of compact with ourselves not to know. We suspect that the implications of what we are doing to the emotional development of our young are so horrifying that we would prefer to remain ignorant, for the veil of denial is easy enough to tear away once we set out to do so.

There are important choices which our society must make if we are to protect our young from the devastating psychological impact of nuclear developments, or to avoid creating a citizenry that experiences little or no stake in the present or the future. At the very least, we need to educate our children to the realities of nuclear energy and weaponry so that they can be helped to overcome at least that aspect of fear which derives from ignorance and which leaves them feeling so powerless. Objective knowledge about the reality of nuclear power and armaments might allow them to take some part in the broader, public debate which must take place. Such knowledge could at least give young people some beginning sense of control over the experience they have of growing up in the nuclear age.

Children seem dangerously unable to connect whatever theoretical understanding of nuclear annihilation they may have with actual current events. Examples of this were television interviews that took place after former President Jimmy Carter's speech concerning the Soviet invasion of Afghanistan. Many high school students offered grimly to "go to war" to "fight the Russians," as if no changes had taken place on the planet since World War II and as if wars could still be fought as these youths had seen them fought in television reruns of World War II films. That war with the Soviet Union carries with it the almost certain implication of nuclear annihilation the students seemed unable to realize.

There are groups in this country seeking to educate themselves, including young people, about the realities of nuclear developments. But the job cannot be left only to those especially interested in this problem. It is the responsibility of the adult generation to give our youth the opportunity truly to participate in the national debate on nuclear issues.

References

1. San-Yu-Sha ND: Summer Cloud: A-Bomb Experience of a Girl's School in Hiroshima. Tokyo, Japan, Hiroshima Jogakuin High School
2. Natural Science Group of the International Peace Bureau: A survivor's story: "friends, please forgive us." Bulletin of the Atomic Scientists, December 1977
3. *Ibid*
4. Lifton RJ: Death in Life. New York, Random House, 1968, p 4
5. *Ibid*, p 506
6. *Ibid*, p 504
7. *Ibid*, p 256
8. Group for the Advancement of Psychiatry: Psychiatric Aspects of Nuclear War, Report 57. New York, 1964, p 224
9. *Ibid*, p 311
10. *Ibid*, p 254
11. *Ibid*, p 256
12. Frank J: Sanity and Survival: Psychological Aspects of War and Peace. New York, Vantage Books, 1967, p 289
13. Escalona S: Children and the threat of nuclear war, in Behavioral Science and Human Survival. California, Science and Behavior Books, 1965
14. *Ibid*, p 204
15. Schwebel M: Nuclear cold war: student opinions and professional responsibility, in Behavioral Science and Human Survival. California, Science and Behavior Books, 1965

16. Law N: Children and war. Association for Childhood Education International, February 1973, p 232
17. Hess R, Torney J: The Development of Political Attitudes in Children. Philadelphia, Friends Peace Committee, 1977
18. *Ibid*, p 221
19. Buergenthal T, Torney J: International Human Rights and International Education. Washington DC, UNESCO, 1976
20. Slovic P: Images of disaster: perception and acceptance of risks from nuclear power, in Perceptions of Risk. Washington DC, National Council of Radiation Protection and Measurements, March 14-15, 1979
21. *Ibid*
22. Luskin J, French CS, Skrable KW, et al: Radiation and life. Presented at the Health Physics Training Thirteenth Mid-Year Topical Symposium. Honolulu, Hawaii, December 10-13, 1979
23. *Ibid*, p 343

CONCLUSION

Despite readily available information about the incalculable effects of a nuclear exchange, the arms race continues. The threat of nuclear destruction through enemy attack, terrorism, human accident, computer error, or power plant disaster creates an environment of fear and imposes stresses upon the human psyche which are without precedent. The production of ever more powerful and sophisticated weapons is itself paradoxically an effort to offset the insecurity that grows out of the distrust which nations experience in relation to one another. But rather than providing security, the uncontrolled proliferation of these weapons increases the likelihood that they will be used and further intensifies the fear which they were meant to allay. Nuclear weapons production is a technological response to what is fundamentally a human emotional, social, and political problem. In this report we have attempted to probe the psychosocial and psychopolitical dimensions of contemporary nuclear developments.

Technological advances have brought new threats as well as new gains to human welfare. In our lifetimes nuclear weapons and nuclear power have heightened enormously the immediate threats and these have not been counterbalanced by the potential future benefits of new energy production, electronic communication, genetic engineering and other technologies. The greatest hope that we shall survive and reap such benefits may be in the growing awareness of the destructive capacity of nuclear weapons by each successive generation.

In Albert Camus' acceptance speech for the Nobel Prize in 1958, he summed up the dilemma of man in the nuclear age:

> We had to fashion for ourselves an art of living in times of catastrophe in order to be reborn before fighting openly against the death instinct at work in our history. Probably every generation sees itself as charged with remaking the world. But its task is perhaps much greater, for it consists in keeping the world from destroying itself.[1]

Our own experiences in working on the Task Force

report certainly have raised more questions than they have answered. We recognize the limitations of what we have said, both in terms of the difficulties in measuring clearly the effects of threats and in comprehending the variety of complex factors that contribute to the problems. We see our work as preliminary, a beginning, not as final or definitive. But we have reached two major conclusions from our own work together. The first of these comes out of our personal experience. The contemplation of nuclear war or of nuclear power disaster in itself is frightening and anxiety provoking, although necessary. We have found that it is essential to share this work with others and to work together in a group setting, rather than to work alone because of the awesomeness and terrible pain of the questions involved. The lack of informed public debate may well stem, in part, from how difficult it is for an individual alone to contemplate these extremely threatening issues. Thus, it is in working together through shared concern that we have found that we have been able to work at all.

The dangers to life and health posed by a nuclear holocaust make it incumbent on all health professionals to strive to prevent this catastrophe. According to a resolution passed by the House of Delegates of the American Medical Association at the annual meeting in June, 1981: "The American Medical Association recognizes the catastrophic danger to all life in the event of nuclear war and supports efforts for the prevention of such a holocaust."[2] The American Medical Association has vowed to inform President Reagan and the Congress of the medical consequences of nuclear war and that "no adequate medical response is possible."

The resolution was part of a Board of Trustees' report approved by the AMA House of Delegates during its winter meeting. Backing up its resolve, the report stressed that in areas hit by a nuclear strike, millions would perish "outright", including health care personnel. Additional millions, it notes, would suffer such severe injuries as massive burns, toxic radiation exposure "without benefit of even minimal medical care."

The report terms "misguided," however, acts by some medical institutions to reject requests by the U.S. Defense Department to join in a plan to allocate a specific number of beds for use in the event of an overseas war.

It also stated that the AMA should stay out of political issues outside its professional expertise, such as national defense.[3]

Mental health professionals can contribute to this goal by presenting information about the psychosocial aspects of the nuclear danger to enable decision makers and the public to incorporate this knowledge into their search for solutions. In contrast to many social and political issues in this country, nuclear weapons, nuclear power, and the arms race have received insufficient bipartisan public debate, perhaps because of the secrecy in which nuclear weapons are shrouded and the fear associated with their awesome potential for destruction. The menace released by developments in nuclear technology may become irreversibly out of control. This report will, we hope, contribute to the prevention of this nightmare.

References

1. Camus A: Nobel Prize acceptance speech. Atlantic 101:34, 1958
2. Anti-nuclear war group proposed. Am Med News, June 19/26, 1981
3. Psychiatric News, February 19, 1982, p 29